Raising the Stakes

From improvement to
transformation in the reform
of schools

Brian J. Caldwell and
Jim M. Spinks

Routledge
Taylor & Francis Group

LONDON AND NEW YORK

Specialist Schools
and Academies Trust
EXCELLENCE AND DIVERSITY

First published 2008
by Routledge
2 Park Square, Milton Park, Abingdon, Oxon OX14 4RN, UK

Simultaneously published in the USA and Canada
by Routledge
270 Madison Ave, New York, NY 10016

*Routledge is an imprint of the Taylor & Francis Group,
an informa business*

© 2008 Brian J. Caldwell and Jim M. Spinks

Typeset in Garamond3 by
RefineCatch Limited, Bungay, Suffolk
Printed and bound in Great Britain by
TJ International Ltd, Padstow, Cornwall

British Library Cataloguing in Publication Data
A catalogue record for this book is available from the British Library

Library of Congress Cataloging in Publication Data
Caldwell, Brian.
  Raising the stakes : from improvement to transformation in
the reform of schools / Brian J. Caldwell & Jim M. Spinks.
    p. cm.
  Includes bibliographical references.
  1. School management and organization.   2. Schools–Decentralization.
3. Educational planning.   4. Educational leadership.   I. Spinks, Jim M.
II. Title.
  LB2805.C234 2007
  371.2 – dc22
  2007007688

ISBN10: 0–415–44045–9 (hbk)
ISBN10: 0–415–44046–7 (pbk)
ISBN10: 0–203–93997–2 (ebk)

ISBN13: 978–0–415–44045–5 (hbk)
ISBN13: 978–0–415–44046–2 (pbk)
ISBN13: 978–0–203–93997–0 (ebk)

Contents

Appendices

    focused self-managing schools   181
2   Self-assessment of knowledge management   184
3   Self-assessment of governance   191
4   Self-assessment of resource allocation   195
5   The Student Resource Package in Victoria   198

    References   203
    Index   211

Illustrations

Figures

Tables

Series foreword
Leading School Transformation

It is now widely accepted that transforming schools is at the heart of system-wide transformation. In order to raise the educational bar while closing the performance gap there has to be continual and relentless attention to improving teaching and learning in our schools. This is unlikely to be achieved unless school leaders are committed to school reform and renewal. This requires leaders who understand the importance of working at both the school and the system level. It also requires leaders who are able to invest in the leadership of others and to share leadership practice widely and deeply.

The Specialist Schools and Academies Trust (SSAT) seeks to give more young people access to a good education by building networks, sharing practice and supporting schools. The Trust's way of working is based on the principle 'by schools for schools' and it is at the heart of a growing network of over 4,500 schools including primary, secondary, special schools and academies in England, as well as schools elsewhere in the UK and internationally. As one of the largest school networks of its kind, it is working with school leaders to explore and trial next practice.

The international arm of the Trust is iNet – International Networking for Educational Transformation. iNet exists to create networks of schools in countries around the world that can innovate and transform schools and school systems. Its prime aim is to secure systematic and sustained change that has a positive impact on young people's achievement. There are currently school networks in Australia, Chile, China, Mauritius, New Zealand, Northern Ireland, South Africa, Sweden, USA (Georgia and Boston) and Wales. iNet schools, institutions and individuals have the opportunity to share innovation and work collaboratively.

I am delighted that SSAT and iNet will be working with Routledge over the next few years to establish the 'Leading School Transformation' series. This is an important series because it will bring together the foremost thinkers and writers in the field of leadership and educational transformation. This is exemplified by the inaugural book by Brian Caldwell and Jim Spinks – *Raising the Stakes: From improvement to transformation in the reform of schools*. It is thought provoking, challenging and very timely. It asks us to think differently about school development, leadership and system reform. It advocates raising the stakes and moving from satisfaction with school improvement to accepting the challenge to transform young people's learning and achievement.

I look forward to reading the other books in the SSAT/iNet series and know that schools all over the world will find this series a source of challenge and inspiration.

Elizabeth Reid
Chief Executive of the Specialist Schools and Academies Trust

Foreword

Very few people who, on hearing the names 'Caldwell and Spinks', would not immediately associate them with 'self-managing schools'. These two educationists have been writing on this topic for over 20 years – a long-term publishing partnership not common in education – developing ideas, sharing ideas and challenging ideas associated with the leadership and governance of schools. Brian Caldwell and Jim Spinks would be worthy recipients of the title of social entrepreneurs, whom they define, following Bornstein (2004), as 'transformative forces: people with new ideas to address major problems who are relentless in the pursuit of their visions, people who simply will not take "no" for an answer, who will not give up until they have spread their ideas as far as they possibly can.' The two are relentless in their pursuit of their vision.

Raising the Stakes, Caldwell and Spinks' fourth book, builds on the authors' previous ideas but challenges educationists to be transformational as they seek solutions to providing the best learning experiences for those in their learning communities. Caldwell and Spinks would be the first to acknowledge that schools in Australia, New Zealand and England, in particular, 'are doing remarkable things with their new authorities and responsibilities.' However, they raise the stakes, up the ante, for self-management by stating in this book that transformational thinking regarding practices, processes and systems, with a focus firmly on the individual learner, is vital if all learners are to realise success in education. They purport that treating students as individuals as well as partners in their learning is key to this process. This present generation of global, digitally literate learners warrants, and will demand, such a participatory bottom-line. This book is not before its time.

Caldwell and Spinks unapologetically call for an alignment and a deployment of resources that ensure the student is at the centre of the process: the new enterprise logic. In fact, throughout *Raising the Stakes*, we are challenged by such words as 'rethinking', 'new approaches', 'working differently', 'the need for a breakthrough', 'radical transformation', 'next practice' – words that leave no doubt that staying the same is not an option. The authors state that success for all students in twenty-first-century schools 'requires some fundamental rethinking about engagement, curriculum, pedagogy and resourcing.' They present working solutions of what this development might look like.

More specifically, Caldwell and Spinks group a school's resources into four broad areas: intellectual capital, social capital, financial capital and spiritual capital. Their research has shown that schools that successfully align at least three out of four of these major areas are those most likely to bring success for their students. Crucially, too, Caldwell and Spinks constantly remind us that five good passes on state examinations is only one part of success; more is needed. The internal factors of school transformation, such as teacher pedagogy, curriculum, and resources, must align with the external factors of the global world within which young people live. In this complex, changing environment, factors such as learning how to learn, engagement, problem-solving and critical thinking are vital. To illustrate this point, Caldwell and Spinks describe how a University of Melbourne project, established to develop a new student-focused resource allocation model, used indicators such as student retention and absence, test scores, post-Year 12 transition, teacher morale and other factors to measure success at the school level.

Raising the Stakes, although visionary, is also grounded and pragmatic. While challenging the status quo, the authors give educational leaders in all roles within the system clear examples of how they can achieve the transformation espoused. For example, in Chapter 1, the authors describe the new enterprise logic of placing students and their learning needs at the centre of strategic thinking and decision-making. In Chapter 8, they present a model of how to do this. A major purpose of the book is to provide a set of tools to assist schools in assessing their progress toward transformation.

To this end, all chapters contain principles or guidelines, strategic intentions or frameworks, or models and diagrams that allow us to see what solutions might look like. However, Caldwell and Spinks ~ present these ideas as a recipe or a definitive answer. Rather, llenge schools to use the tools to develop their own policy and practices so that these reflect their own communities, values and beliefs, strategic directions and unique local needs. A clear framework is established at the beginning of each chapter and there is a coherent flow of ideas throughout the book. Stories in Chapter 10 show how schools have found ways of aligning at least three of the four kinds of capital to achieve success for students. International examples are given of schools' and school leaders' responses to the challenge of personalising learning for every student. The appendices contain self-assessments for knowledge management, governance and resource allocation.

Raising the Stakes follows Hutt's lead in its demand that schools have, as their 'default position', the aim that *all* children – even the Bridgets, Kyles and Coreys – successfully complete school and do not fall through the cracks. I am sure we can all relate to Caldwell and Spinks' examples of individual children and their learning journeys. The authors acknowledge that while it is not unusual for a child to be 'saved' in our schools, such a situation is rarely the default position. This is why they stress raising the stakes to ensure success for every student. Bishop's cutting-edge research and development in New Zealand with indigenous students certainly backs this position. Bishop's work shows that teachers who successfully focus on the individual student's learning experience by changing pedagogies, assessment practices and curriculum to engage, connect and relate to the learner as a partner in the process also have success with all learners. Caldwell and Spinks give examples on page 80 of how such learners describe such 're-imagined schools'.

Caldwell and Spinks also call for learning communities of the talent force. They believe that building intellectual capital requires not only hiring the best people, but also continuing to ensure that all people 'who work in or for the school are at the forefront in terms of their professional capacity.' Building the individual and shared capacity of teachers is paramount, and the building of social capital is a necessary part of this process. The authors set this claim within a definition that posits the 'school has social capital to the extent that it is part of a mutually supporting network of individuals, organisations, agencies and institutions in the public and private sectors, in education and in other fields.' Only then can the talent force operate with the common moral purpose of providing the best learning experiences for young people.

Although Caldwell and Spinks talk about teaching and pedagogy, rather than the learning relationship, they leave us with no doubt, in regard to their model for alignment, that they mean 'creating unprecedented opportunity for learners and learning'. Teachers will quite rightly say, 'How can we do this with 30 students in our classes? How can we personalise learning? How can we connect and engage with so many students?' The answer? Not by doing more of the same. We cannot achieve this aim by relying on old systems and practices, something we know all too well. There needs to be new approaches to the allocation of resources. Teachers need the time to get to know students as individuals, to build a relationship with them, to work alongside them in the development and achievement of targets, goals, aspirations, dreams. Those in positions of responsibility – head teachers, governors, advisers, other educational leaders – need the courage to stand by their convictions for change.

Let me give you a personal example here. I was recently part of regional workshops conducted with secondary leaders throughout England and Wales that had as their aim rethinking the pastoral care of students. Some schools shared how they had worked through major transformation of their pastoral systems to ensure every student had personalised learning relationships with their teachers. However, I frequently heard leaders proclaim, 'But I am not sure I have the courage to do that!' Engaging in this process does take courage, but courage is easy to hold fast to when the moral conviction that 'this is making a positive difference to students' lives' is evidenced and is at the forefront of professional practice. Caldwell and Spinks give many practical examples of how schools have approached this challenge.

Raising the Stakes does not propose systems built on deficit models. Instead, the authors present a strong social justice agenda and consistently argue for success for all in all settings. Theirs is not an either/or approach: it is both high quality and high equity. Caldwell and Spinks believe all students can learn, and that all students have capabilities and the capacity for learning. If the student is the unit of learning, then there is acknowledgment of the individual and the central role that culture and background play in learning. The authors also recognise the importance of consultation and partnership with family in the learning relationship. The challenge to educators is to remove the impediments to students' learning, and Caldwell and Spinks believe the most important way to achieve this is to make all settings *great* settings for young people.

Raising the Stakes asks us to seek different ways of viewing the places of learning in communities; different educational and social imaginaries; new ways of thinking about education. Transformation will require a shift in thinking about priorities and the allocation of resources. There may need to be changes to the way timetabling is approached in schools so that this practice does not dictate curriculum but supports curriculum pathways and enables access to programmes that suit students' individual 'nature, needs, interests, targets, aptitudes and aspirations'.

Caldwell and Spinks do, however, state that a twenty-first century place of learning will recognise it cannot be all things to all persons and that an important part of aligning spiritual capital is about attaining coherence of values and beliefs, and developing a strength of moral purpose so that the learning community has a shared purpose. They also acknowledge that one size does not – *cannot* – fit all. One school may not sufficiently meet the needs of a particular student, and other places of learning might more successfully meet the individual needs of learners in the wider community. Creative uses of space, place and time through the opportunities technology affords will be important to this process. Such leaders of transformation will need to be ethical leaders and, as such, system leaders, who realise the importance of having an influence greater than on their own school. They will also be people who recognise that all of the students in the neighbouring schools and, indeed, globally are important to sustainability and to the long-term good of the community.

Caldwell and Spinks define transformation at the beginning of Chapter 3. They state, 'A school has been transformed if there has been significant, systematic and sustained change that secures success for all of its students.' They could not put it more clearly than that. They believe that 'Failure in educational reform is to a large degree the failure to achieve alignment.' Achieving the alignment of the four kinds of capital – intellectual, social, financial and spiritual – 'calls for outstanding governance'. (Interestingly, Caldwell and Spinks seldom use the word leadership in this book.) They go on to say, 'that while alignment is important, it should include a capacity for creativity, innovation, exploring the boundaries and developing a new alignment,' and, importantly, they offer a model to support such an alignment.

The authors also acknowledge and build on colleagues' work. They critique the present, but offer an alternative and give exemplars. They are pragmatists. They are in touch with school leaders. They accept that some exploration is in its infancy and that further work is needed. But throughout *Raising the Stakes*, they never veer from their initial tenet – there must be transformation in education for all students to achieve their aspirations and have a purposeful future. Can we rise to their challenge?

Jan Robertson
Director, London Centre for Leadership in Learning,
Institute of Education, University of London, UK

Preface

We believe it is time to raise the stakes in the transformation of schools. There are five reasons. The first derives from the meaning of transformation, which we consider to be significant, systematic and sustained change that secures success for all students in all settings. Governments around the world have subscribed to this view for decades but nations still fall short of its achievement, except in a relatively small number of schools. It is time for delivery to be an issue on which governments stand or fall. The second concerns the manner in which schools are supported. There are reservoirs of resources that have not been drawn on to the extent that is possible or desirable because of the limited view that is held about the support of public education. If the reservoirs of resources are considered to be forms of capital, then it is time that we increased the capital of schools: financial capital, intellectual capital, social capital and spiritual capital. The third relates to the limited range of people who have a serious stake in the success of schools. It is time that every individual, organisation and institution became a stakeholder. The fourth is concerned with failure to fully network knowledge about how transformation can be achieved. This book renews the call for researchers, policymakers and practitioners to work more closely in this regard. The fifth reason is that a focus on school improvement has got us only so far. It is time to raise the stakes and move from satisfaction with improvement to accepting the challenge to transform.

There is now persuasive if not irrefutable evidence that all students can achieve success, even under the most challenging of circumstances, if all of the resources that are required to support the effort are made available to schools, where they are deployed strategically in the passionate and purposeful pursuit of such an outcome. This has been a truly remarkable breakthrough, and our aim in this book is to share information about how it has been achieved and to show how all schools can do the same. A precondition is that schools be self-managing and that their leaders be allowed to lead.

This is our fourth book for an international readership that describes what is occurring around the world when significant and systematic authority and responsibility are decentralised to schools and that offers guidelines for schools and school systems that seek to move in this direction. These books about self-managing schools span two decades and our fourth is concerned with what has been accomplished and remains to be done when the focus shifts to the student.

The book is intended to stand alone, so that the reader need not return to its predecessors to gain an understanding of where we are coming from. It may be helpful, nevertheless, to briefly re-trace the journey and explain why we have selected the themes that are highlighted in the pages that follow. That is the purpose of this preface.

We are approaching the 25th anniversary of the research and development project that became the foundation of our work. The starting point was a project of national significance in Australia that identified highly effective schools, in a general sense and in the manner in which they allocated their resources. The project was conducted in 1983 and was funded by the Australian Schools Commission. It came at a time of growing global interest in school effectiveness and school improvement. The outcome was the identification of a model for self-management that was evident in its clearest and most readily describable form at the school in Tasmania at which Jim Spinks was principal. A workshop programme was prepared for use in Victoria where more authority and responsibility were being decentralised to schools, and training was required for school councils, principals and teachers, and for students in secondary schools. More than 50 workshops were conducted for about 5,000 people from 1984 to 1986. The workshop materials and guidelines for take-up were packaged together and published by the Education Department of Tasmania under the title *Policy-making and Planning for School Effectiveness: A Guide to Collaborative School Management* (Caldwell and Spinks, 1986).

It soon became evident that the book and the research and development programme on which it was based were relevant to developments in other countries, especially in England where interest was building in the local financial management of schools and the Education Reform Act of 1988 was taking shape. The book was updated to take account of these developments and published for an international market under the title of *The Self-Managing School* (Caldwell and Spinks, 1988). It became a key resource in scores of workshops in England and New Zealand, most of which were led by Jim Spinks, and as a guide to practice as thousands of schools took up their new authorities and responsibilities. Interest continued to build in our own country, Australia, and in places like Hong Kong.

We learnt much from schools as self-management took hold, especially in how leadership was exercised where successful implementation had occurred. This led to *Leading the Self-Managing School* (Caldwell and Spinks, 1992) which became a guide for a further thrust to self-management in Victoria under the rubric of Schools of the Future, wherein about 90 per cent of the state's education budget was decentralised to schools for local decision-making. We were involved in two important aspects of implementation. Firstly, we were members of the Education Committee of the School Global Budget Research Project charged with determining how money would be delivered to schools. Per capita and needs-based components were incorporated in the funding formula along similar lines to what had been pioneered in Edmonton, Canada more than a decade earlier, a practice that Brian Caldwell had studied in the late 1970s. Secondly, the processes and outcomes of Schools of the Future were the subject of a five-year study initiated by the primary and secondary principals' associations and known as the Cooperative Research Project. Three professors from the University of Melbourne were part of the project team: Hedley Beare, Brian Caldwell and Peter Hill. While a robust data base was still some way off, findings from surveys of school principals and case studies by doctoral candidates enabled the team to map the links between the capacities that came with self-management and learning outcomes for students.

It was soon time to update accounts of the practice and incorporate findings on impact on learning and so we wrote *Beyond the Self-Managing School* (Caldwell and Spinks, 1998). By 1998, self-management had passed the 'tipping point' in England, New Zealand and Victoria, and some school districts in Canada, especially Edmonton, and the United States. Impetus for further development came with the election of the Blair New Labour government in England in 1997, which chose to extend the self-management reform of the Conservative government to the point that, like Victoria, 90 per cent of public funds were decentralised to the school level. A change in government in Victoria in 1999 saw further extension to 94 per cent.

There were two important features of *Beyond the Self-Managing School* that are pertinent to this fourth book. One was that we set it in the context of major reforms that were gathering momentum around the world. We referred to these as 'tracks for change' and three were identified. Track 1 was 'building systems of self-managing schools', describing the trend in an increasing number of countries. Track 2 was 'unrelenting focus on learning outcomes'. Track 3 was 'creating schools for the knowledge society', driven to a large extent by developments in information and communications technology. School systems differed in the extent to which they had moved down each 'track'. This momentum continues to build, but it is in respect to the second track ('unrelenting focus on learning outcomes') that this fourth book responds, because there are heightened expectations that all students should succeed, as illustrated in initiatives such as No Child Left Behind (USA), Every Child Matters (UK) and Nurturing Every Child (Singapore). Personalising learning is part of a powerful agenda in most instances.

A second feature of *Beyond the Self-Managing School* was the formulation of 100 'strategic intentions', offered as a guide to schools and school systems that were nurturing a capacity for self-management and that sought to move further down the tracks for change set out above. A review of developments in different places reveals that many, but still a minority, of schools have successfully addressed these intentions. In this fourth book we wish to draw from successful experience, especially in the context of personalising learning, and offer guidelines for practice where implementation is still in its early stages.

Our experience since 1998 has provided further insights. Jim Spinks has played a key role in updating and refining the funding formula for schools in Victoria to make it more sensitive to the needs, interests, aptitudes and aspirations of students and to achieve a greater degree of equity in funding through the Student Resource Package. He worked with his wife Marilyn Spinks, also a former principal, through their All Across the Line consultancy to provide advice on the funding of special needs students. They have provided expert advice on the funding mechanism in South Australia as its system of government schools has moved further down the track of self-management.

Following his time as Dean of Education at the University of Melbourne, Brian Caldwell undertook a review of developments in self-managing schools and wrote three pamphlets based on 19 workshops conducted in 2005 in Australia, Chile, England and New Zealand under the auspices of the Specialist Schools and Academies Trust (SSAT), for whom he serves as an associate director. He found that practice had moved beyond initial conception to the point that it was time to 're-imagine the self-managing school'. He described the 'new enterprise logic of schools' and studied the phenomenon of 'exhilarating leadership', referring to the role of principals and other school leaders who were succeeding in transforming their schools. The three pamphlets were brought together, updated and published as *Re-imagining Educational Leadership* (Caldwell, 2006).

Our work came together in a new series of pamphlets and workshops, sponsored by the SSAT, which addressed the issue of how an agenda for personalising learning could be resourced if schools were to be transformed. Workshops were conducted in Birmingham, Darlington, London (two workshops) and Manchester. The pamphlets drew on the work described above and insights gleaned from 19 more workshops conducted by Brian Caldwell around Australia in mid-2006 for the Australian College of Educators, based on *Re-imagining Educational Leadership*. Presentations by policymakers and practitioners at national conferences of the SSAT in 2005 and 2006 yielded more valuable information, as did site visits and case studies.

We were struck by the impact of the education reforms of the Blair New Labour government, especially in respect to the agenda for personalising learning and the networking of knowledge among schools. We were concerned that the funding mechanism for self-managing schools in England was still based on the Age Weighted Pupil Unit (AWPU) when a student-focused model was clearly a requirement for personalising learning. We intend this book to be a guide to achieving a breakthrough in this regard.

It is timely that we bring together our new understandings of what can be achieved in self-managing schools when the intent is to secure success for all students in all settings. We found it sobering to re-read a passage in *Beyond the Self-Managing School*, written for publication in 1998, some 10 years after the 1988 Education Reform Act in the UK. We surmised that 10 years was 'the amount of time it takes to move a nation'. We continued:

> Taken together, allowing for overlapping developments on the three tracks, it is likely that at least two decades will have elapsed since the decision to restructure systems of public education to the time when there is general consensus that all students are receiving a high quality education and are learning well, with this learning and the efforts of teachers and other professionals supported by state-of-the-art technology.
>
> (Caldwell and Spinks, 1998, pp. 14–15)

We are still short of the goal of all students in all settings 'receiving a high quality education', and we are approaching the end of the two decades we foresaw as being required to achieve such an outcome. Time is short, and we hope that this book, which draws extensively on the experience of those who have succeeded, will help us get there.

We acknowledge the critiques of self-management that have been mounted from time to time. Most were addressed in *Beyond the Self-Managing School*. The most insightful are those that question the impact on learning and we hope that the critics and commentators can learn, as we have done, from those who have made the links. We are encouraged that governments of all persuasions accept that a focus on the student demands a significant and systematic capacity for local decision-making, and that the overwhelming majority of principals and other school leaders would not wish to return to more centralised arrangements, although they resent the lack of support for their work in some settings and the mountain of unnecessary paperwork that is often generated.

We extend our appreciation to a number of organisations and individuals who have assisted in this endeavour. The Specialist Schools and Academies Trust commissioned the pamphlets, organised the workshops and invited our contributions to national conferences. We acknowledge, in particular, the following principals in the UK who shared their knowledge: Tony Barnes, Headteacher of Park High; Sir Dexter Hutt, Executive Headteacher of Ninestiles Community School; Roger Lounds, Headteacher at Lymm High School; Dr Elizabeth Sidwell, Principal and Chief Executive Officer of the Haberdashers' Aske's Federation; and Michael Wilkins, Headteacher of Outwood Grange College. In Australia, site visits were arranged and information was provided by several principals including Jim Davies, Australian Science and Mathematics School in Adelaide; Mary Dorrian, St Monica's Parish Primary School in Canberra; and Gerry Schiller, Glen Waverley Secondary College in Melbourne. In Chile, Nilda Sotelo Sorribes, Principal of Sociedad Educacional Maria Luisa Bombal in Vitacura (Santiago), provided information for the study of the unique approach to governance and self-management at her school.

Brian Caldwell extends special thanks to Dr Jessica Harris, Director of Research at Educational Transformations, who contributed to our understanding of policy and practice in Finland and assisted with school studies in Australia. Jim Spinks extends his appreciation to the Department of Education and Training in Victoria, for whom he has served as a consultant on the Student Resource Package and the support of special needs students, and the South Australian Secondary Principals Association, who invited his expert contribution on matters related to the funding of secondary schools. His wife and partner in All Across the Line, Marilyn Spinks, was a valued colleague in each instance.

We are delighted that Routledge is publishing our fourth book on self-managing schools, with publisher Anna Clarkson providing the same encouragement and support as Malcolm Clarkson, founder of Falmer Press, did for the first. Series Editor Professor Alma Harris agreed to make this the first of the iNet (International Networking for Educational Transformation) series.

We invite readers to join us in taking up the challenges and dealing with the paradoxes of a new era of self-managing schools. The closer we come to recognising that the student is the most important unit of organisation, the more we need to take on board the implications of globalisation in education, including the notion of the student as a global citizen. The stronger the trend to self-managing schools in systems of public education, the more schools network with other schools and organisations in the public and private sectors, working laterally as much if not more than within traditional lines of authority and support. The more we understand the importance of money to fund the personalising of learning, the more we see schools draw on other sources of support, acknowledging that spiritual capital, intellectual capital and social capital are as important as financial capital. We know that local decision-making is more sophisticated and demanding than ever before, and so we embrace best practice in governance to ensure that there is alignment of these four forms of capital. Resistance to oppressive standards-based accountability measures is justified, but it is essential to embrace the best of student-focused data banks that enable schools to identify and respond to the needs, interests, aptitudes and aspirations of students. We have learned these things from policy makers and practitioners who are committed to and have been successful at securing success for all students in their jurisdiction. We look forward to all schools succeeding in this quest. It is then that we can celebrate the transformation of schools.

Brian J. Caldwell
Melbourne, Victoria
Jim M. Spinks
Paradise, Tasmania
June 2007

Chapter 1

A new view of self-management

Introduction

No reform in education can succeed without appropriate resources to support the endeavour. This means that initiatives such as Every Child Matters in England, No Child Left Behind in the United States, and the Blueprint for Government Schools in Victoria (Australia) are certain to fail if the level and mix of resources are not appropriate.

Traditionally such a statement would be assumed to mean more money is needed from government to reduce class sizes, or fund a programme of in-service training for teachers about a preferred approach to curriculum or pedagogy, or provide a new pot of money as an incentive for schools to take on a new project related to one or more aspects of the reform. All of these may be desired by policymakers, who include these time-honoured approaches in their election campaign announcements. They would be welcomed by practitioners, because well-designed initiatives in school improvement must be funded one way or another, and the size of the school budget is sometimes (mistakenly) seen as an indicator of success.

The focus on money alone as the chief resource for schools has not resulted in expectations being achieved to any great extent. While his message is often greeted by puzzlement or even anger, the Hoover Institution's Eric Hanushek found that increases in funding for schools have had, with few exceptions for some programmes, little impact on educational outcomes over many decades. His conclusion could not be clearer: 'The aggregate picture is consistent with a variety of other studies indicating that resources alone have not yielded any systematic returns in terms of student performance. The character of reform efforts can largely be described as "same operations with greater intensity"' (Hanushek, 2004, p. 12).

Governments have despaired when their apparently well-conceived programmes have not succeeded, sometimes blaming teachers who are perceived as unresponsive or incompetent or both. Schools are frustrated because they feel their best efforts have not been supported. Schools and school systems continue to search for the magic formula for the allocation of funds among schools and within schools so that expectations can be achieved.

These disappointments are largely the result of a narrow view of resources and adherence to a status quo view of the way schools and school systems should be led and managed. They reflect what may be described as 'old enterprise logic of schools'. This is similar to Hanushek's explanation of lack of impact cited above: 'same operations with greater intensity'. The 'new enterprise logic' (Caldwell, 2006) and the adoption or adaptation of the OECD's (Organisation for Economic Cooperation and Development) 're-schooling' scenarios (OECD, 2001a) will yield a different and much richer view of what we mean by resources. Money is important, but the key issues are concerned with the range of resources and how each is deployed. What are the most important resources if expectations are to be achieved? Limited success in the past, and a chief source of despair, derives from a view that the key unit of organisation is the school system or the school or the classroom, especially the last of these. It means that an important indicator for governments at election time, or for teacher unions at all times, or for teachers who find that their best efforts are not appreciated, is the student–teacher ratio. Success is indicated by the number of new teachers who have been hired, or the extent to which student–teacher ratios have been lowered, and some broad brush indicators of learning outcome, such as average performance on international tests such as those conducted in the Programme for International Student Assessment (PISA) or the Trends in Mathematics and Science Study (TIMSS), or a national or local benchmark like the number of students receiving five good passes in the General Certificate of Secondary Education (GCSE) (England) or the percentage of students who reach a particular level in the curriculum and standards framework, as measured by the Achievement Improvement Monitor (AIM) (Victoria).

What is needed is a new mechanism to allocate funds when the key unit of organisation is the student, not the classroom or school or school system. What is needed is a view of resources that pays more than lip-service to intellectual capital, one that accounts more accurately and comprehensively for the knowledge and skills of every person who supports the learning enterprise, and ensures that all who work in or for the school are at the forefront in terms of their professional capacity. What is needed is the application of all of the resources of a community, not just government and not just money, and this is where the notion of social capital comes in. It has been under-valued and under-utilised in the past. There is still no systematic way to measure the level of social capital that supports the school. What is also needed is a sense of urgency, accompanied by an unprecedented campaign of action, to replace the appalling facilities in which much of the learning and teaching occurs in many countries. Resources in the form of infrastructure still reflect a nineteenth-century factory or industrial model, or 'the old enterprise logic'.

The good news is that this broader view of resources is now being adopted in some countries as governments and the wider community reach the end of their tether. England is good example of where there is now a deeper understanding of what is required. Following the White Paper (Secretary for Education and Skills, 2005), new legislation provides every school with an opportunity to acquire a trust, employ its staff and manage its assets. Trusts may support a number of schools which will acquire the flexibility of specialist schools and academies. The tipping point has been passed as far as specialist secondary schools are concerned, with a consistent gain over non-specialist schools in achievement in the GCSE, with benefits being greatest in schools in challenging circumstances. Local authorities will have an important strategic role in establishing and expanding schools, responding to the needs and aspirations of students and parents, and helping to drive up standards.

In the remaining pages of Chapter 1, some underlying assumptions are addressed, summarised at the end as 'first principles'. These assumptions concern the agenda for transformation, the personalising of learning, the self-management of schools, the new enterprise logic of schools and the emergence of philanthropy and social entrepreneurship as a key driving force for achieving success in trusts and the building of social capital.

Transformation

It is important that the scale of the challenge is appreciated. This is not allocation of resources for improvement. It is the allocation of resources for transformation. Transformation is significant, systematic and sustained change that secures success for all students in all settings, thus contributing to the well-being of the student and society. What this achievement is about, and how it is measured, varies from setting to setting and is invariably contentious.

Transformation is an appropriate word because such an outcome ('all students in all settings') has never been accomplished in any society in the history of education. It has, however, been accomplished in some settings. Success in these instances involved particular approaches to the allocation of resources. A major purpose of this book is to identify the principles that underpin these approaches to help build a capacity to do the same in all schools and school systems.

Personalising learning

At the heart of the theme of 'all students in all settings' is the importance of personalising the learning experience. Shoshanna Zuboff and Jim Maxmin coined the concept of 'new enterprise logic' in describing what is required in every organisation, public and private. As far as schools are concerned, they declared that 'parents want their children to be recognised and treated as individuals' (Zuboff and Maxmin, 2004, p. 152). Tom Peters included education in his general call to 're-imagine': 'Teachers need enough time and flexibility to get to know kids as individuals. Teaching is about one and only one thing: Getting to know the child' (Peters, 2003, p. 284).

The case for transformation through personalising learning was made in England in the *Five-Year Strategy for Children and Learners* (DfES, 2004a).

'Over the last 60 years, a fundamental recasting of industry, employment, technology and society has transformed the requirement for education and training – not only driving the education system, but introducing new ideas about lifelong learning, personalised education, and self-directed learning. And the story has been of taking a system designed to deliver a basic minimum entitlement and elaborating it to respond to these increasingly sophisticated (and rapidly changing) demands.

'The central characteristic of such a new system will be personalisation – so that the system fits the individual rather than the individual having to fit the system. This is not a vague liberal notion of letting people have what they want. It is about having a system which will genuinely give high standards for all – the best possible quality of children's services, which recognises individual needs and circumstances; the most effective teaching at school which builds a detailed picture of what each child already knows and how they learn, to help them go further; and, as young people begin to train for work, a system that recognises individual aptitudes and provides as many tailored paths to employment as there are people and jobs. And the corollary of this is that the system must be freer and more diverse – with more flexibility to help meet individual needs; and more choices between courses and types of providers, so that there really are different and personalised opportunities available' (DfES, 2004a, p. 4).

The Five-Year Strategy contained a range of approaches to personalising learning, including the use of information and communications technology, individualised assessment for diagnosis, the planning of learning experiences for each student, and the provision of children's services to support the work of teachers as they endeavour to meet the needs of each learner.

As further illustration in another setting, the former head of the Department of Prime Minister and Cabinet in Australia, Michael Keating, made the following observation: 'The reforms of public administration affecting service delivery stemmed fundamentally from public dissatisfaction with many of the services provided. The major problems were their lack of responsiveness to the particular needs of the individual client or customer . . . society has become more educated and wealthy and its individual members have developed greater independence and become more individualistic . . . This individualistic society is both more demanding and more critical of service provision' (Keating, 2004, p. 77).

Self-managing schools

It is inconceivable that an agenda for transformation through personalising learning could be achieved without a high level of decentralisation in decision-making. Schools should be self-managing.

> A self-managing school is a school in a system of education to which there has been decentralised a significant amount of authority and responsibility to make decisions related to the allocation of resources within a centrally determined framework of goals, policies, standards and accountabilities.
> (Caldwell and Spinks, 1998, pp. 4–5)

Critics or sceptics have suggested that self-management has not had an impact on learning. This may have been true in the early stages when capacities at the school level were limited, especially in the absence of a strategy to make the link to learning and the data base was weak. Evidence is now strong. Ludger Woessmann, formerly at the University of Kiel and now Head of the Department of Human Capital and Structural Change at the Ifo Institute for Economics in Munich, undertook a comprehensive study of why students in some countries did better in TIMSS, and found a powerful connection between decentralisation of decision-making to the school level and student achievement (Woessmann, 2001). It is a connection that has been affirmed in subsequent results in PISA (Programme in International Student Assessment). Andreas Schleicher, Head of the Indicators and Analysis Division at OECD, identified decentralisation as one of several policy levers for student achievement (Schleicher, 2004). He found that, in the best performing countries:

- Decentralised decision-making is combined with devices to ensure a fair distribution of substantive educational opportunities.
- The provision of standards and curricula at national/sub-national levels is combined with advanced evaluation systems.
- Process-oriented assessments and/or centralised final examinations are complemented with individual reports and feedback mechanisms on student learning progress.
- Schools and teachers have explicit strategies and approaches for teaching heterogeneous groups of learners.
- Students are offered a variety of extra-curricular activities.
- Schools offer differentiated support structures for students.
- Institutional differentiation is introduced, if at all, at later stages.
- Effective support systems are located at individual school level or in specialised support institutions.
- Teacher training schemes are selective.
- The training of pre-school personnel is closely integrated with the professional development of teachers.
- Continuing professional development is a constitutive part of the system.
- Special attention is paid to the professional development of school management personnel.

More evidence about the link to learning is reported elsewhere (Caldwell and Spinks, 1998; Caldwell, 2002; Caldwell, 2003; Caldwell, 2005; Caldwell, 2006).

The new enterprise logic of schools

A review of developments in the self-management of schools by Caldwell (2006) found that best practice had outstripped initial expectations. It had become a key mechanism in efforts to achieve the transformation of schools. Nine workshops over nine weeks in four countries in the first half of 2005 revealed how success had been achieved. The concept of 'new enterprise logic' was adapted from Zuboff and Maxmin (2004) and its key elements are listed below. Together they constitute a new image of the self-managing school.

1 The student is the most important unit of organisation – not the classroom, not the school and not the school system – and there are consequent changes in approaches to learning and teaching and the support of learning and teaching.
2 Schools cannot achieve expectations for transformation by acting alone or operating in a line of support from the centre of a school system to the level of the school, classroom or student. Horizontal approaches are more important than vertical approaches, although the latter will continue to have an important role to play. The success of a school depends on its capacity to join networks or federations to share knowledge, address problems and pool resources.
3 Leadership is distributed across schools in networks and federations as well as within schools, across programmes of learning and teaching and the support of learning and teaching.
4 Networks and federations involve a range of individuals, agencies, institutions and organisations across public and private sectors in educational and non-educational settings. Leaders and managers in these sectors and settings share a responsibility to identify and then effectively and efficiently deploy the kinds of support that are needed in schools. Synergies do not just happen of their own accord. Personnel and other resources are allocated to energise and sustain them.
5 New approaches to resource allocation are required under these conditions. A simple formula allocation to schools based on the size and nature of the school, with sub-allocations based on equity considerations, is not sufficient. New allocations take account of developments in the personalising of learning and the networking of expertise and support.

6   Knowledge management takes its place beside traditional management functions related to curriculum, facilities, pedagogy, personnel and technology.
7   Intellectual capital and social capital are as important as other forms of capital related to facilities and finance.
8   New standards of governance are expected of schools and the various networks and federations in which they participate. These standards are important in the likely shift from dependence and self-management to autonomy and self-government.
9   Each of these capacities requires further adaptation as more learning occurs outside the school, which is one of several major places for learning in a network of educational provision. The image of the self-managing school continues to change in different settings.
10 The sagacity of leaders and managers in successful self-managing schools is likely to be the chief resource in preparing others, if transformation in a short time and on a large scale is the goal (Caldwell, 2006, pp. 71–2).

This book takes up the theme of item 5 in this list. Particular attention is given to items 6 and 7, which refer to resources that have been under-utilised in efforts to achieve change on the scale of transformation, namely, intellectual capital and social capital; and to item 8 on new standards in governance.

Intellectual capital or intellectual assets refer to the 'talent, skills, know-how, know-what, and relationships – and machines and networks that embody them – that can be used to create wealth' (Stewart, 2002, p. 11) or, in the case of schools, 'to enhance learning'. Knowledge management in item 6 refers to the creation, dissemination and utilisation of knowledge for the purpose of improving learning and teaching and to guide decision-making in every domain of professional practice. Building intellectual capital and sustaining it through a comprehensive approach to knowledge management are the hallmarks of successful organisations in a knowledge society. Few schools have developed a systematic approach beyond the selection of qualified teachers and relying on occasional in-service days. It is a theme of this book that the creation of intellectual capital and state-of-the art approaches to knowledge management are essential for transformation and are key requirements in the acquisition and allocation of resources at the school level.

Fukuyama (1995) defined social capital as 'the ability of people to work together for common purposes'. A school has social capital to the extent that it is part of a mutually supporting network of individuals, organisations, agencies and institutions in the public and private sectors, in education and in other fields. As in other organisations in western society, social capital for schools became weak in the second half of the twentieth century (Putnam, 2000). The challenge is to support schools as they seek to build their social capital. An impressive achievement in England is the way more than 2,600 of about 3,100 secondary schools have secured cash or in-kind support from thousands of individuals, organisations, agencies and institutions when they became specialist schools. New legislation extended the opportunity for schools or networks of schools to secure the support of trusts.

These are dramatic developments, considering that schools in England had little support of this kind barely a decade ago. In many respects they are benefiting from the rise of philanthropy which has its counterparts in other countries. *The Economist* (2006a) documented the trends: 'Giving away money has never been so fashionable among the rich and famous'. Bill Gates led the way in providing US$31 billion to the Bill and Melinda Gates Foundation to support health and education, including a large grant to Cambridge University. Many school projects are supported, including an initiative to create smaller schools in the United States. Among developed countries, the United States leads the way in philanthropy, followed by Canada, Britain, the Netherlands, Sweden, France, Japan, Germany and Italy. 'Britain's government has recently been trying to foster the philanthropic spirit, and other European countries are starting to follow suit. Even in China, the government seems keen to build up a non-profit sector that caters to social needs' (ibid.).

There are many shortcomings in traditional approaches to philanthropy. A preferred approach calls for a major role for 'social entrepreneurs' who can operate within an infrastructure that is 'the philanthropic equivalent of stock markets, investment banks, research houses, management consultants and so on' (ibid.). Moreover 'philanthropists need to behave more like investors' who seek to maximise their 'social return'. This was the style of the transforming philanthropies set up by Carnegie and Rockefeller. *The Economist* documented the rise of the 'social entrepreneur' and highlights the work of Ashoka, a global organisation that invests in the field. It notes that 'social entrepreneurs now rub shoulders with the world's business and political elite at the World Economic Forum in Davos' (ibid.). The field is now taken seriously in academic circles, as illustrated in the endowment of the Skoll Centre for Social Entrepreneurship at Oxford University. Harvard Business School entered the field in 1994.

Bornstein (2004) wrote the engagingly titled *How to Change the World: Social Entrepreneurs and the Power of New Ideas*. He described social entrepreneurs as 'transformative forces: people with new ideas to address major problems who are relentless in the pursuit of their visions, people who simply will not take "no" for an answer, who will not give up until they have spread their ideas as far as they possible can' (p. 1). He contends that 'social entrepreneurs have existed throughout the ages. St Francis of Assisi, founder of the Franciscan Order, would qualify as a social entrepreneur, having built multiple organisations that advanced social pattern changes in his field' (p. 2). Bornstein estimates that in the 1990s, the number of registered international citizen organisations increased from 6,000 to 26,000 (p. 4).

The Economist (2006a) concluded that 'much remains to be done before today's beneficent billionaires can claim to follow in the footsteps of such giants of giving as Carnegie, Rockefeller and Rowntree'. It called for better measurement of outcomes, greater transparency and improved accountability.

Secondary schools in England are benefiting from the rise of philanthropy, and many will have experienced its shortcomings. There is little doubt that providing a place for philanthropy and social entrepreneurship is part of 'next practice' in acquiring and allocating resources in schools of the twenty-first century, especially within the framework of legislation that provides for trusts and more autonomy for schools.

Chapter outline

Chapter 1 concludes with a summary of 'first principles' for the acquisition and allocation of resources for self-managing schools when the student is considered the most important unit of organisation and the goal is to secure success for all students in all settings. Chapter 2 describes the 'core principles' that should underpin 'next practice' in the transformation of schools. Particular attention is given to resource allocation as an aspect of good governance in education, zero tolerance of corruption, the centrality of quality in teaching, knowledge management, building capacity for leadership, facilities that meet requirements for learning in the twenty-first century and needs-based funding.

Chapter 3 describes four kinds of capital that are the wellsprings of the resources required to secure transformation. It is explained how these must be aligned, each with the other and together, on the needs, interests, aptitudes and aspirations of students. A model for alignment is described. Alignment will only occur if there is effective governance. A case for a new alignment in education is presented, arguably the first 'grand alignment' since the late nineteenth and early twentieth centuries. Examples are provided from several nations of progress in securing alignment and the constraints presented in some settings in securing it. Chapter 4 explains and illustrates the concept of intellectual capital, describes two new approaches for schools that seek to achieve transformation, describes an instrument for assessing capacity in an important aspect of intellectual capital (knowledge management) and offers benchmarks from Australia and England that will assist schools to make judgements on the strength of this form of capital.

Chapter 5 defines governance, explains the connections to social capital and financial capital, makes clear that good governance is necessary in alignment, and describes an instrument for self-assessment of a capacity for good governance and another that focuses on the acquisition and allocation of resources. An example is provided of good practice in governance in new arrangements in England for the federation of schools. The chapter concludes with a set of 'enduring principles', complementing 'first principles' (Chapter 1) and 'core principles' (Chapter 2).

Chapters 6 to 9 are concerned with financial capital and the role it plays in securing success for all students. Financial capital is critical if strength in the other domains is to be attained. Expressed simply in the case of intellectual capital, adequate funding is needed if the best professional talent is to be secured. Chapter 6 canvasses a range of issues in the alignment of financial capital and learning outcomes. Developments in Australia and England are summarised. Chapter 7 describes and illustrates an approach to the development of student-focused allocation models that deliver funds from the centre of a school system to a school. Particular attention is given to work in Victoria. Guidelines are offered for addressing the achievement of 'high quality' and 'high equity'. Also included is a description of approaches for the funding of students with special education needs.

Chapter 8 describes and illustrates a student-focused planning model. Whereas Chapter 7 was concerned with the allocation of funds to schools, Chapter 8 deals with the deployment of funds within schools. A pre-condition for deployment which helps secure success for all students in all settings is that schools have a model or template for plans that respond to the needs, interests, aptitudes and aspirations of students. Illustrations are provided from two secondary schools in England.

Chapter 9 explains how student-focused planning works in practice. Given the assumption that the most important unit of organisation is the student and the goal is to secure success for all students in all settings, particularly under challenging circumstances, the chapter is organised around descriptions of three students with dramatically different needs, interests, aptitudes and aspirations. In each instance, strategies are derived in relation to curriculum and pedagogy and how the costs of support should be addressed. We explain how the budget of a school should be structured if learning is to be personalised and the school is to be transformed. Drawing on the breakthrough work of Fullan, Hill and Crévola (2006), we conclude the chapter with a call for greater precision in the gathering and utilisation on a daily basis of data on student progress.

Chapter 10 returns to the theme of alignment and the importance of aligning the four forms of capital considered in preceding chapters (spiritual, intellectual, social and financial). Alignment is made effective through good governance. There is an unrelenting focus on the student. Examples are provided of practice in three schools from three systems of education in Australia (two secondary and one primary), one school in England (secondary) and one in Chile (a primary-secondary school). Attention is drawn again to the importance of appropriate facilities if alignment is to be effective.

Recommendations for policy and practice are provided in Chapter 11. These are intended for ministers of education, senior officers in systems of education, principals and other leaders in schools and their immediate communities, professional associations and teacher unions, and leaders in other settings in the public and private sectors who are key stakeholders in securing success in schools. We inject a note of urgency in these recommendations, for reforms in education have been underway for two decades or more in some places and outcomes still fall short of the expectation that success should be secured for all students. It is time to raise the stakes and set all schools on the path to transformation.

First principles

Several principles emerge from the analysis in this chapter. They are considered to be 'first principles' to be observed in policy and practice.

1   A transformation in approaches to the allocation and utilisation of resources is required if the transformation of schools is to be achieved.
2   The driving force behind the transformation of schools and approaches to the allocation of resources is that henceforth the most important unit of organisation is the student, not the classroom, not the school and not the school system. It is a pre-requisite that schools be self-managing.
3   Exclusive reliance on a steadily increasing pool of public funds, with much of the effort focused on mechanisms for the allocation of money, will not achieve transformation.
4   While there is increasing recognition of their importance, there are currently few accounts of good practice in building intellectual and social capital in schools, and it is important that new approaches to the allocation and utilisation of resources, as well as to governance, take account of their value.
5   Next practice in providing resources to schools must take account of the rise of philanthropy and social entrepreneurship.

These principles are simply the starting point. They are considered here to be 'first principles'. 'Core principles' are addressed in Chapter 2 and 'enduring principles' in Chapter 5. The three sets of principles are brought together in Appendix 1.

Core principles for next practice

Introduction

This chapter contains the 'core principles' that should underpin the allocation of resources to schools, the acquisition of resources by schools, and the allocation of resources within schools, in a new view of the self-managing school wherein the student is the most important unit of organisation and the goal is to secure success for all. Seven domains are explored: resource allocation as an aspect of good governance, zero tolerance of corruption, the centrality of quality in teaching, knowledge management, building capacity for leadership, facilities that meet requirements for learning in the twenty-first century and needs-based funding. Core principles are derived in each instance, as summarised in a set of ten at the conclusion of the chapter. They should guide 'next practice' in the resourcing of schools.

Resource allocation as an aspect of good governance

The best approaches to the allocation of resources will meet the highest standards of governance. This is true at all levels in schools and school systems. A definition of governance and a framework for assessment of its practice were developed in a project of the Human Resource Development Working Group of Asia Pacific Economic Cooperation (APEC) on *Best Practice Governance: Education Policy and Service Delivery* (Department of Education, Science and Training, 2005). APEC represents about one-third of the world's population. Fourteen of its 21 members contributed case studies to the project.

Drawing from work by the International Institute of Administrative Sciences (1996) the report of the project noted that governance is a broader notion than government, whose principal elements include the constitution, legislature, executive and judiciary. It involves interaction between these formal institutions and those of civil society. Civil society is considered here to be the network of mutually supporting relationships between government, business and industry, education and other public and private sector services, community, home and voluntary agencies and institutions. Traditional approaches to governance in public education have minimised such interaction but, as suggested in Chapter 1, there is recognition that social capital in civil society is an importance resource, so a broader view of governance is required in the formulation of 'next practice'.

The APEC project involved the design of a framework for the assessment of governance in education. Drawing on the work of the International Institute of Administrative Sciences (1996) and the World Bank Group (2001) broad indicators were provided in four domains (purpose, process, policy, standards). There are several elements in each domain and these are explored in Chapter 5.

Zero tolerance of corruption

It may puzzle or even offend that the issue of corruption is raised in this book. Nevertheless, we are in good company, for it was also the subject of a major report of the International Institute for Educational Planning (IIEP) of UNESCO (Levačić and Downes, 2004). The report was prepared by Rosalind Levačić, an internationally-regarded expert in school finance, and Peter Downes, former President of the Secondary Heads Association (SHA) in England, who helped pioneer the local financial management of schools in Cambridgeshire. Case studies were provided of formula funding for schools under conditions of decentralisation in Australia (Victoria), the United Kingdom (England), Poland (Kwidzyn and Swidnik) and Brazil (Rio Grande do Sul).

The reason for the study was stated in the following terms:

> Given that the proportion of the national budget devoted to education is significant for both developed and developing countries, it is essential that public funds be directed effectively and used for the purposes for which they are allocated. The misuse of public funds is a serious matter both in terms of ethical and criminal implications of the abuser and in terms of the deprivation of funding inflicted on students.
>
> (Levačić and Downes, 2004, p. 15)

The focus was on practice in systems of self-managing schools. Particular attention was given to transparency, the accurate collection of data, the avoidance of fraud and the need for a range of auditing procedures at different levels. Few instances of fraud were uncovered in the study.

Several recommendations were made and these are consistent with indicators of good governance. They were concerned with training, preparing manuals of financial procedures, removing opportunities for collusion, designing an agreed format for financial reporting across the system, local monitoring that is frequent and independent of the head (principal) and administrative staff, the use of independent auditors, external checking of statistics that are used in determining allocations and clarity in explanations of funding formulae so that they can be readily understood by all stakeholders. The report concluded that 'formula funding for schools reduces the potential for corruption by increasing transparency as the amount each school should receive and the basis for this is public knowledge' (p. 145). The report contains a useful appendix that sets out the financial regulations for schools administered by the Cambridgeshire County Council.

The report noted that 'England and Victoria have the systems with the greatest level of delegation with Victoria offering the clearer and more stable needs-led funding methodology'. It stated that 'the recent (2003) reform of funding in England failed to achieve the full version of needs-led funding that many had hoped for' (p. 131). In contrast, Victoria took the already 'clearer and more stable' approach to a new level, as described and illustrated in Chapters 6 and 7.

The centrality of quality in teaching

The foregoing was concerned with two basic but critical considerations. Approaches to the allocation of resources must conform to standards for good governance and there must be zero tolerance of corruption in the process. However, the most important issue to be addressed is what kinds of resources make a difference if transformation is intended and there is a commitment to ensure that the student is the most important unit of organisation.

Simply increasing the amount of money allocated to schools may not have an impact, and this was the starting point of Chapter 1. The work of Eric Hanushek was cited. He concluded that the most important resource was the quality of teaching. 'The available evidence does indicate that improvement in the quality of the teaching force is central to any overall improvement. And improving the quality of teachers will almost certainly require a new set of incentives including selective hiring, retention, and pay' (Hanushek, 2004, p. 22). In his often cited conclusion, that increases in the level of funding in recent decades have had minimal impact on learning outcomes, he is always careful to acknowledge that the link between additional resources and improvements in learning has been demonstrated under some circumstances, especially for students with special education needs, including those with moderate to severe disabilities, and in the early years.

Simply increasing the amount of money to compensate for the personal circumstances of students, such as the socio-economic status of their families, may also have little impact on learning outcomes. As Hanushek described it, this may involve 'same operations with greater intensity'. The issue is the extent to which additional resources will improve the quality of teaching.

An example of best practice may be found at Bellfield Primary School, which serves the Melbourne suburb of West Heidelberg, a community characterised by high levels of aggression, gambling, alcohol and drug abuse. Enrolment is about 220 and remains steady. About 80 per cent of children's families receive the Education Maintenance Allowance (an indicator of socio-economic status), nearly 60 per cent of students come from single parent families, and slightly more than 20 per cent are from non-English speaking backgrounds. Many of these students are refugees from Somalia. There is an indigenous (Aboriginal) enrolment of about 20 students. It is one of the most disadvantaged schools in Victoria. The 1996 Triennial Review revealed that over 85 per cent of students were behind state-wide benchmarks in literacy and numeracy.

Transformation at Bellfield Primary School is reflected in the performance of students on tests that show remarkable improvement, bringing the school close to the essence of the definition of transformation, namely, securing success for all students in all settings, especially under challenging circumstances. Results for Bellfield on state-wide tests in the Preparatory Grade and in Grades 1 and 2, as summarised in Table 2.1, illustrate what has been accomplished. Noteworthy are comparisons with schools in similar settings, with all schools across the state and with results in 1998.

Transformation was achieved by building the capacity of staff. It called for outstanding leadership, notably by former principal John Fleming. A visit to the school reveals a quiet, safe orderly

Table 2.1 Transformation of learning outcomes at Bellfield Primary School

Preparatory Grade: Percentage reading with 100 per cent accuracy at Level 1

Bellfield 2004	Like schools 2004	State-wide 2004	Bellfield 1998
97.4	58.5	67.5	33.3

Grade 1: Percentage reading with 100 per cent accuracy at Level 15

Bellfield 2004	Like schools 2004	State-wide 2004	Bellfield 1998
100	26.3	35.9	34.6

Grade 2: Percentage reading with 100 per cent accuracy at Level 20

Bellfield 2004	Like schools 2004	State-wide 2004	Bellfield 1998
83.3	38.7	47	30.6

environment. A teaching vacancy results in scores of applications to fill the post. Each year there are literally hundreds of visitors who come to found out how the transformation was achieved (more information in Caldwell, 2006).

A key feature of Table 2.1 is the performance of students at Bellfield compared to those in 'like schools' (schools with a similar profile of socio-economic indicators). If socio-economic circumstance can be overcome at Bellfield, it can be overcome in similar settings if similar strategies to build the capacity of staff prove as successful. A first step is rejection of the view that socio-economic circumstance necessarily leads to low achievement, even if research has shown that it is an important predictor of such an outcome. Indeed, approaches to the allocation of resources that simply direct additional resources to schools to compensate for socio-economic circumstance may be ineffective, as they clearly have been in the case of many of the 'like schools' whose performance is summarised in Table 2.1.

It is worthwhile to briefly review the evidence on the relative impact of quality of teaching and socio-economic circumstance. Ken Rowe, who chaired the National Inquiry into the Teaching of Literacy for the Australian Government, is expert in this field. He cited two studies. One, by Peter Tymms, was of results in England for the GCSE and A-levels.

In every case more variance [among measures of student achievement] was accounted for at the department level than between schools, and the proportion of variance at the class level was more than at the departmental level. A general principle emerges from data such as these and that is the smaller the unit of analysis and the closer one gets to the pupil's experience of education, the greater the proportion of variance explicable by that unit. In accountability terms the models indicate that teachers have the greatest influence.

(Adapted from Rowe, 2004, p. 9)

The other study cited was by John Hattie, who drew on an extensive review of literature and a synthesis of findings in more than half a million studies and reached a similar conclusion. Percentages of explained variance were students (50), teachers (30), home and peers (5–10) and schools and principals (5–10). He concluded that:

we should focus on the greatest source of variance that can make the difference – the teacher. We need to ensure that this greatest influence is optimised to have powerful and sensationally positive effects, but they must be exceptional effects. We need to direct attention at higher quality teaching, and higher expectations that students can meet appropriate challenges – and these occur once the classroom door is closed and not by reorganising which or how many students are behind those doors, by promoting different topics for teachers to teach, or by bringing in more sticks to ensure they are following policy.

(cited in Rowe, 2004, pp. 12–13)

The approach at Bellfield was consistent with the findings of Tymms and Hattie.

There are important implications for those concerned with the allocation of resources at all levels. Governments and other authorities must invest in policies that attract, prepare, place and reward outstanding people to serve in schools. Schools must have a capacity to select those whose talents meet the unique mix of and priorities among learning needs at the local level. Once in post, working conditions must be of such a standard that people will be retained in the profession, rather than seek an exit within a few years of appointment, as is the case in some nations, including Australia and the United Kingdom. Some of these conditions are included in other domains explored below. All of these considerations are a far cry from policies and practices in recent years, where just about any qualified person can be employed to work in a depressing environment that was designed for a factory era of schooling.

An exemplar in these matters is Finland (Harris, J., 2006). One of several factors accounting for the success of Finland in PISA is the quality of its teachers. Finnish teachers are highly valued and well paid professionals who are expected to have high levels of pedagogical expertise and flexibility in order to achieve success with students who learn in heterogeneous groups. Applications to tertiary education studies are so high that just 10–12 per cent of applicants are accepted in teacher education programmes. Only those who demonstrate outstanding academic ability and personal qualities are accepted. All teachers are required to have a masters degree in either pedagogy or the subject that they wish to teach.

Knowledge management

It will require leadership of the highest order at every level of government and in universities to achieve an expectation that all teachers should hold a masters degree before taking up their appointments. In the absence of such a qualification, and the assumed capacities that follow, schools must become powerful learning communities if teachers are to be at the forefront of professional knowledge. They should remain so, even when these high standards of initial teacher education are achieved. Principals and other school leaders shall require a capacity to develop a comprehensive approach to knowledge management, described in more detail in Chapter 4.

More schools are building a powerful capacity for professional learning. Some are approaching this in comprehensive fashion through the creation of an institute. Wesley College in Melbourne, the largest non-government school in Australia, has established such an entity. Launched in 2005 with eminent scientist Sir Gustav Nossal as its patron, The Wesley Institute aims to 'gather the best minds, encourage the best talent, promote the best research and explore the best ideas to further the cause of education and to lead to the best possible outcomes for teaching and learning'. In carrying out its work, the Institute will be a laboratory of innovation where ideas are generated, translated, evaluated and implemented; an observatory of excellence, monitoring the world's best practice for implementation; and a conservatory of ideas embodying the memory, heritage and identity of the College as a leader in educational innovation. It is intended to build a capacity to impact on classroom learning outcomes within the school; contribute to the wider educational community, nationally and internationally, and influence the broader development of society. It will conduct seminars and conferences, publish a professional journal and develop partnerships with other institutions and educational and philanthropic organisations. It is intended that there be substantial external funding to support the enterprise.

It is evident that occasional in-service training does not constitute the kind of knowledge management that is required for success in the transformation of schools. It is also evident that resources must be provided or acquired and then allocated to support the effort. Small schools, indeed most schools, will join networks to share knowledge, address common problems or pool resources. Consistent with the new enterprise logic of schools set out in Chapter 1, these networked learning communities must be led and resourced.

Building capacity for leadership

It is apparent that the role of the principal is more complex and demanding than ever before. This is occurring at the same time that concerns are raised about the number of vacancies and the paucity of applicants. In Victoria, *The Privilege and the Price* (Department of Education and Training, 2004) reported on workload in government (public) schools and its impact on the health and wellbeing of the principal class (principals and assistant principals). Regarding workload, for example, the number of hours per week for principals in Victoria was similar to that for headteachers in England, as reported in a survey at about the same time, being about 60 hours. In both places, this is well above the average for leaders and managers in other professional fields in several European nations (about 45 hours per week). The report contained disturbing evidence of the impact on the emotional and physical wellbeing of principals.

Even more disturbing is the evidence from England about the number of vacancies and the number of acting appointments to the position of headteacher. The issue is not the number of positions falling vacant each year. On average, a school seeks a new head about once every seven years, which means about 14 per cent advertise each year. The number of schools advertising in 2005 was 12 per cent. Of deeper concern is that more than one-third of schools were not able to make an appointment after the initial advertisement. Education Data Surveys (EDS) reported that re-advertisement reached record levels. EDS's John Howson suggested that: 'the 2005 results are alarming, especially for secondary schools. In all the time I have been conducting this survey, I cannot recall the problem being this bad'. The seriousness of the situation is affirmed in a report of the National Audit Office (NAO) that blamed the shortage of headteachers for holding back progress in the most challenged schools (Smithers, 2006).

The interim report of a two-year study conducted by the National Association of Head Teachers (NAHT), the Eastern Leadership Centre (ELC), the University of Cambridge, the National College for School Leadership (NCSL) and the Hay Group (NAHT et al., 2005) found that 'the number of quality candidates to choose from is often seen as too small or nonexistent'. It drew attention to the fact that headteacher salaries had risen on average by 34 per cent between 1998 and 2003. Salaries exceed £100,000 per annum for heads of secondary schools in London; a level likely to make them the highest paid principals of public schools in the world. The report canvassed a range of good practices in recruitment, drawing on approaches from England and other countries. At the same time, it acknowledged that recruitment and appointment of headteachers is an international concern.

Principals everywhere resent the mountain of paperwork they are required to deal with. It goes without saying that this must be reduced to an absolute minimum, but the larger issue of approaches to knowledge management of schools is raised. Part of the deep support to be expected of centralised services is to furnish every school and every leader with a state-of-the-art computer-based system to assist every aspect of school operations, including curriculum, pedagogy, assessment, accounting and accountability. Some schools are doing this well from their own resources, but it is a capacity that ought to be built for all. School leaders are lagging far behind their counterparts in health care and far behind airline services when it comes to managing information about the individual. How much more important it is in schools, where the focus is personalising learning. The principal's office ought to be a paperless office.

A related issue is the amount of support for principals. There can be few enterprises as large as a typical secondary school or a big primary school where the chief executive does not have a personal assistant and several managers to deal with business and finance. Why is there not such support for principals of these schools, or for principals in networks of smaller primary schools, or however networks of schools are configured? It is inexplicable that such support is not included in the basic package of support for leaders of schools in the public sector, when it is taken for granted for their counterparts in the private or independent sector. The notion of a 'package' is stressed, because the way in which the resource is used will vary from school to school. Some principals may not seek additional personal assistance or require a business manager, or they may choose to outsource the support.

When it comes to the exercise of leadership across a system, the traditional approach has been to appoint successful principals to formal positions in a central office, from where they are expected to influence developments across the system, in whole or in part. It remains the most widely-practised approach to system leadership. It has generally worked well. In terms of the scenarios developed at OECD (2001a), it is part of a 'status quo' scenario ('bureaucratic systems continue'). It is an approach that is consistent with the old enterprise logic. The preferred scenarios ('schools as core social centres' and 'schools as focused learning organisations') call for a high level of professional networking. An approach that is consistent with these preferred scenarios and the new enterprise logic is for successful principals to remain in their posts but exert influence across all or part of a system, rather than leave for an appointment in a central office. This is a new view of the 'system leader', defined by David Hopkins, HSBC iNet Chair in International Leadership at the Institute of Education in London, in the following terms:

> "System leaders" are those headteachers [principals] who are willing to shoulder system leadership roles: who care about and work for the success of other schools as well as their own. System leaders measure their success in terms of improving student learning and increasing achievement, and strive to both raise the bar and narrow the gap(s). They look both into classrooms and across the broader system, they realise in a deep way that the classroom, school and system levels all impact on each other. Crucially they understand that in order to change the larger system you have to engage with it in a meaningful way.
>
> (Hopkins, 2006)

Hopkins includes the nurturing of 'system leaders' in a range of strategies that support a vision of 'every school a great school', adapting to education the terminology of Jim Collins in *From Good to Great* (Collins, 2001). There are major implications in this analysis and in the directions foreshadowed as far as the allocation of resources to schools and within schools is concerned. These must be addressed if leadership is to be sustained at a level that is required for success in the transformation of schools.

Facilities that meet requirements for learning in the twenty-first century

The majority of schools in nations where this book will be read were built decades ago to a design that is ill-suited to the needs of the twenty-first century. In many cases, the facilities are dilapidated and should be bulldozed and replaced. The following is a worst case account of what might be found on a visit to such schools. Regardless of the physical condition of the buildings, there is little flexibility in the use of space, classrooms are frequently overflowing with different technologies, corridors are being used for learning and teaching in small groups, teachers are hidden behind a mountain of books in overcrowded staffrooms or are working in isolated fashion in their classrooms, meetings of and with parents occur in makeshift facilities, and there are few fit-for-purpose working spaces for professionals other than teachers. Portable or demountable classrooms have become permanent fixtures, providing crowded and unhealthy spaces for teachers and students in seasonal extremes.

The effects go beyond those described. An increasing proportion of teachers are leaving the profession within a few years of graduation. Apart from the demands of teaching under conditions more challenging and complex than in the past, their physical working conditions compare poorly with those in most private schools, or those for their peers who work in other professions. Indeed, they are inferior to those found in almost any business.

The drift of students to private schools can be explained in part by school design and the facilities suffered by students and staff. Many private schools have the resources to create schools to a twenty-first-century design, leaving behind the industrial model of the last century. Such a comparison is readily made by parents who will exercise choice when they can afford the fees, as an increasing proportion of parents can, given the continuing strength of the economy. Some observers may find it puzzling that schools built on factory lines can still be found in many communities, when the factories upon which they were modelled have long departed the scene.

It is encouraging that some countries are doing something about this situation. The aim of the Building Schools for the Future (BSF) initiative in England is to rebuild or renew every secondary school over a 10–15 year period. A 50:35:15 formula has been adopted: 'new building' for 50 per cent of floor area; 'major refurbishment/remodelling' for 35 per cent and 'minor refurbishment' for 15 per cent. Public private partnerships (PPP) constitute an important strategy for achieving this outcome in a relatively short time. Construction shall be state-of-the-art and shall take account of curriculum and pedagogy that will lie at the heart of school education for the decades ahead, with due consideration for developments or requirements in underperforming schools, extended or full service schools, specialist schools, academies, ICT and workforce reform.

Needs-based funding

The allocation of resources from central sources in systems of self-managing schools through mechanisms known variously as 'global budgets' or 'student resource packages' are as important as ever. Determining the 'funding formula' is a complex and continuous challenge and the outcomes each year are eagerly awaited in schools. The money in these allocations is the major item on the income side of the annual budget.

Allocations to schools include a per capita component, with weights that differ according to stage of schooling, and needs-based components that reflect student and school characteristics. Good progress was made in the 1990s in several countries (see Levačić and Ross, 1999 for a summary of approaches in Australia, Canada, England, New Zealand, the United States and Wales).

To a large extent, allocations for the per capita component reflect historical approaches and old enterprise logic, especially in respect to a class rather than student focus and assumptions about student–teacher ratios. The challenge is to identify best practice in schools where there has been transformation and a shift in focus from the class to the student. Allocations in many elements of the student needs component are based on personalising learning where moderate to severe disabilities are involved. Indeed some special schools are models of approaches to personalising learning. Allocations that reflect school characteristics invariably take account of size and economies of scale; location, especially in remote or rural settings, and stage and specialisation in schooling, where there are different resource requirements.

Needs-based funding is problematic when efforts are made to compensate for disadvantage associated with socio-economic circumstance. It is in this regard that quality of teaching, knowledge management and social capital are critically important. The case of Bellfield Primary School was cited earlier in the chapter as an example of how these matters were addressed and transformation was achieved. Levels of achievement in 'like schools' are relatively low, and no amount of additional funding will make a difference unless the building of professional capacity is modelled along the same lines as Bellfield. It may be that schools that achieve transformation along these lines will relinquish some elements of funding as success is secured.

Chapter 7 describes emerging practice in the needs-based funding of schools. Chapter 8 describes and illustrates a student-based planning model for use in schools that seek to secure success for all students. Chapter 9 illustrates how the model works in practice where the intention is to personalise learning.

Core principles

The following 'core principles' summarise the themes explored in Chapter 2. They are intended to help shape 'next practice' in the allocation of resources.

1 Approaches to the acquisition, allocation and utilisation of resources should conform to criteria for good governance in respect to purpose, process, policy and standards.
2 There should be zero tolerance of practices that may lead to corruption in matters related to the acquisition, allocation and utilisation of resources.
3 Quality of teaching is the most important resource of all, and school systems and other organisations and institutions should place the highest priority on attracting, preparing, placing, rewarding and retaining the best people for service in the profession.
4 Schools should have the authority to select and reward the best people in matching human resources to priorities in learning and teaching and the support of learning and teaching.

5 A human resource management plan is a necessary component of the school plan for the acquisition, allocation and utilisation of resources.

6 A knowledge management plan to ensure that all staff reach and remain at the forefront of professional knowledge is a necessary component of plans to achieve transformation, and resources must be allocated to support its implementation.

7 There should be a plan for systematically building the social capital of the school, with provision for participation in and contribution to networks of support in a whole-of-government and whole-of-community approach.

8 Principals and other school leaders should have salary packages that reflect the complexities of their roles, and be resourced for full executive and managerial support, with state-of-the-art systems to eliminate unnecessary paperwork.

9 Most schools should be re-built or replaced to provide facilities appropriate for learning in the twenty-first century, recognising that these are required to attract and retain the best people in the profession.

10 Formula funding remains the largest component of resources to support schools, but more work is needed to base per capita and needs-based elements on best practice in transformation rather on historical patterns that reflect old enterprise logic.

Chapter 3

Alignment

Introduction

A school has been transformed if there has been significant, systematic and sustained change that secures success for all of its students. Some schools can provide evidence of transformation by referring to data on student achievement. They will show how current high levels of achievement represent a dramatic improvement on results in the past, and that these high levels have been sustained. Transformation on this scale is particularly meritorious when it has been achieved in challenging circumstances. How was such a transformation achieved? What does a school that makes a commitment to transformation need to do to achieve success? How does a school that has made such a commitment know if it is on the road to success?

It is easy to confuse means and ends when it comes to making a claim that a school has been transformed. A run-down facility with an obsolete nineteenth- or twentieth-century design might have been replaced by a state-of-the-art building that has all the features deemed to be important in a school for the twenty-first century. There may have been a transformation in the building but no transformation in achievement.

A school may have re-designed its curriculum so that each student can find a pathway that matches interest and aspiration, but the opportunity for personalising learning may not be there because there is no change in pedagogy. The school may have highly qualified teachers in an academic sense – all may have masters degrees with specialisation in particular disciplines – but staff continue to use the same one-approach-suits-all when it came to styles of learning and teaching. Alternatively, staff may have the know-how to make change to curriculum and pedagogy, but neither curriculum nor pedagogy are valued by, or are relevant to, the community the school seeks to serve.

The point we make is straightforward. There must be strength in every domain but, more importantly, each of these strengths must be aligned with every other strength. To illustrate, the design of state-of-the-art facilities must be consistent with the design of a relevant curriculum that must, in turn, be delivered through a range of pedagogical practices by professionals with the knowledge and skill to accomplish the task, with each of these consistent with the needs of society and the expectations of the community. Plans and budgets should enable this alignment. A major purpose of this book is to explain and illustrate how strength can be developed in each domain and how progress in building that strength can be measured. Expressed another way, how can the school be assured it is on track for transformation?

Alignment

A simple analogy is presented by Robert Kaplan and David Norton in *Alignment* (Kaplan and Norton, 2006). They invite us to consider rowing crews in a river race:

> Although each shell contains strong, highly motivated ath-letes, the key to their success is that they row in synchronism. Imagine a shell populated by eight highly conditioned and trained rowers, but with each rower having a different idea about how to achieve success: how many strokes per minute were optimal and which course the shell should follow, given wind direction and speed, water current and a curvy course with multiple bridge underpasses. For eight exceptional rowers to devise and attempt to implement independent tactics would be disastrous.
>
> (Kaplan and Norton, 2006, p. 1)

The same image applies to any enterprise in education and certainly to schools. These questions may be posed: Does the school have 'strong, highly motivated athletes' (a talented team of teachers and other professionals)? Do they 'row in synchronism' (teachers and other professionals aligned in their efforts to secure success for all students) or is it a matter of 'each rower having a different idea about how to achieve success'?

Like all images, the image of the rowing crew is concerned with only one facet of what it takes to achieve success. In this instance it is 'alignment'. In other aspects of professional practice, a different image is more appropriate to the extent, for example, that a diversity of strengths or a high degree of artistry may be required. The image for diversity might be of players in a symphony orchestra. If creativity and improvisation are valued, the image might shift to a jazz band.

Kaplan and Norton described a study of practice in three kinds of corporation in which five key processes were assessed: mobilisation of effort to achieve change; capacity to translate strategy into action; alignment of different units in the organisation; motivation of employees and quality of governance. One kind of corporation belonged to the authors' 'hall of fame', being exemplars in the use of their highly regarded balanced scorecard approach. A second reported significant benefits from the approach although they were not in the class of the 'hall of fame'. A third reported few benefits after using the approach. The three kinds of corporation were ranked on the basis of their performance in the five key processes and, in each instance, the rank order was the same: 'hall of fame' performed best, followed by 'high benefit' and then, last, 'low benefit'. The greatest gap in performance was for alignment of the different units in the organisation. The authors conclude that 'understanding how to create alignment in organisations is a big deal, one capable of producing significant payoffs for all kinds of enterprises' (Kaplan and Norton, 2006, p. 3). After alignment, the largest gap in performance was for governance.

There is little doubt that similar results would be found in the analysis of performance in many schools, where different units are expected to work together in the implementation of strategies to achieve success. Adopting the language of Kaplan and Norton, it is likely that schools in the 'hall of fame' as far as transformation is concerned will be strong in each of the five key organisational processes, including alignment of different units within the school. In this book we extend the concept to include alignment of the schools with what can be broadly described as societal expectations for schools.

The concept of alignment is consistent with theory on leadership and management. The distinction that John Kotter makes between the two is helpful, as summarised in Table 3.1.

Leadership involves those activities in the right hand column of

Table 3.1 Alignment in leadership and management

Management	Leadership
Planning and budgeting	Establishing direction
Organising and staffing	Aligning people
Controlling and problem-solving	Motivating and inspiring
Producing a degree of predictability	Achieving change

(Based on Kotter, 1990)

Table 3.1. It is important to note that leadership does not involve actions on the part of one person only. There may be many leaders. Leadership is, or should be, 'distributed' in most organisations (Harris, A., 2005). Leadership calls for establishing the direction of the enterprise and then ensuring that all who work in it are aligned in their efforts. The image of the rowing crew offered by Kaplan and Norton may be invoked along with clichés such as 'all singing off the same song sheet' or 'getting the right people on the bus'. Leadership involves motivating and inspiring those who are engaged in the endeavour. The purpose is to achieve change. If no change occurs, either none was expected, in which case no leadership was required, or there was a failure in leadership. It goes without saying, especially in education, that the desired change should have moral purpose. Moral purpose is evident in the view of transformation that has been adopted: securing success for all students in all settings, thus contributing to the wellbeing of the student and society.

There is alignment of management processes, as listed in the left column of Table 3.1, with these elements in leadership. If leadership involves establishing direction, then moving in that direction calls for planning and the preparation of a budget. If people are to be aligned, then an important aspect of management is securing the best people for the task (staffing) and getting some structure in the operation (organising). A measure of control is required in matters such as implementation of the budget. Problems will arise and these must be resolved to keep the enterprise on track. While change with moral purpose is desired, all who work in the organisation yearn for stability and predictability in the way they go about it.

A model for alignment

We propose a model for alignment if transformation is to be achieved. The student lies at its heart. This is as it should be, given that the purpose of transformation is to secure success for all students in all settings. Four domains are included, and there must be alignment one with the other. Above all, there must be alignment with the interests of students and the goal of transformation. Four kinds of capital constitute the domains: intellectual capital, social capital, spiritual capital and financial capital. Securing alignment between these different types of capital calls for outstanding governance. The entire enterprise must succeed in a context of change – local, national and international. The stakes are high. If schools are transformed in the sense under consideration in this book, it opens up an era of unprecedented opportunity for learners and learning. This is a global challenge.

The model is illustrated in Figure 3.1. The following bullet points contain brief descriptions of the four kinds of capital, along with a definition of governance.

- *Intellectual capital* refers to the level of knowledge and skill of those who work in or for the school, all of whom should be at the forefront of knowledge and skill. We prefer the concept of 'talent force' to 'workforce'.
- *Social capital* refers to the strength of formal and informal partnerships and networks involving the school, parents, community, business and industry, indeed, all individuals, agencies, organisations and institutions that have the potential to support and, where appropriate, be supported by the school.
- *Spiritual capital* refers to the strength of moral purpose and the degree of coherence among values, beliefs and attitudes about life and learning. For some schools, spiritual capital has a foundation in religion. In other schools, spiritual capital may refer to ethics and values shared by members of the school and its community.
- *Financial capital* refers to the monetary resources available to support the school as it seeks to achieve transformation, securing success for all students. It is acknowledged that some schools are in more challenging circumstances than others, so the notion of needs-based funding is embraced.
- *Governance* is concerned with the formal decision-making processes of the school and their interaction with civil society,

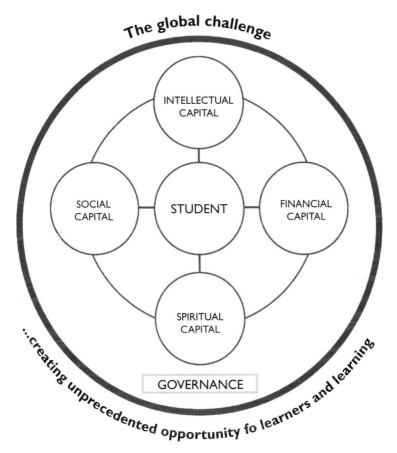

Figure 3.1 A model for alignment.

which comprises the network of mutually supporting relationships with government, business, industry, other services in the public and private sectors, community, home and voluntary agencies and institutions.

Why capital?

The choice of the word 'capital' to describe the domains to be aligned warrants an explanation. A major purpose of the book is to provide a set of tools to assist the school assess its progress to transformation. The reader might be expecting an extended list of indicators on curriculum, teaching, learning and assessment, as well as data on outcomes. These are important, but whether a high level of performance on each can be attained depends on the resources on which the school can draw. It is in this respect that the concept of capital is helpful.

Capital has several meanings that are relevant in this context. According to the Merriam-Webster online dictionary, capital refers to 'accumulated goods devoted to the production of other goods' or 'a store of useful assets or advantages'. Intellectual capital, for example, may be viewed as 'accumulated goods' ('the level of knowledge and skill of those who work in or for the school') devoted to the 'production of other goods' (state-of-the-art curriculum and pedagogy leading to 'success for all students'). High levels of capital in each of the four domains constitute 'a store of useful assets or advantages'.

Assessing the degree of alignment in a school

A sense of the degree of alignment in a school can be obtained by inviting the perceptions of key stakeholders on the matter. This can be done formally or informally as part of a planning or professional development activity. An example of its use in the latter was in a workshop of school leaders organised by the Specialist Schools and Academies Trust (SSAT) in London in December 2006. Participants were principals, deputy principals and bursars of affiliated secondary schools. They were invited to rate on a scale from 1 (low) to 10 (high) the strength of each kind of capital in their schools and the degree of alignment. They were briefed on the concept of alignment and each kind of capital. Responses are summarised in Table 3.2.

Mean ratings were modest, in the range 5.6 to 6.3 for the four kinds of capital, and lowest at 5.1 for the degree of alignment.

Table 3.2 Assessing the degree of alignment in schools: ratings by participants in a London workshop of school leaders on a scale from 1 (low) to 10 (high); 23 participants

Item	Intellectual capital	Social capital	Spiritual capital	Financial capital	Degree of alignment
Mean	5.8	6.3	5.7	5.6	5.1
Range	4–9	2–9	2–8	2–8	3–8

Participants provided a wide range of ratings in each instance. Noteworthy is the higher mean rating for the strength of social capital (6.3), possibly reflecting the significant developments in specialist secondary schools in England. At the time of the workshop, more than 80 per cent of approximately 3,100 secondary schools had formed partnerships with business and industry (broadly defined) in areas of specialism. There is no counterpart to such a development in comparable countries. All schools in England have governing bodies of parents and other members of the community with significantly greater powers than in the past.

Participants were also invited to nominate the part of the model where it is most difficult to secure alignment. Spiritual capital and financial capital were mentioned most frequently, the former to secure agreement among disparate groups and the latter to ensure money is allocated to priorities for learning. It was noted in discussion that different ratings would be given for different parts of the school, and that trends were as important as assessments at a fixed point of time. It was agreed that ratings of the kind provided in this kind of activity are subjective, but a useful starting point for strategic conversation. Finer-grained assessments of intellectual capital, financial capital and governance are discussed in Chapters 4 and 5, with related instruments contained in the appendices.

It's time for a new 'grand alignment'

Scientists have coined the term 'grand alignment' to refer to an event that occurs about every 20 years when all planets are in alignment on the same side of the sun. It is often the subject of scaremongering, with alarming predictions of volcanic eruptions, earthquakes and tsunamis, if not the end of civilisation as we know it. The event passes without discernible impact. There is similarity with expectations for many reforms in education that occur every decade or so. Some would argue that, like the grand alignment in astronomy, these are recurring events that have no significant impact or leave little of lasting value. It is no wonder that many in the education profession are cynical about change.

There is an important difference between astronomy and education. Alignment in the former has no impact. Alignment in the latter has the potential to have powerful impact, but it has rarely occurred. Failure in educational reform is to a large degree the failure to achieve alignment.

The last grand alignment

A case can be made that there has been no 'grand alignment' in education since the late nineteenth century, when everything from school design to curriculum to the organisation of schools and school systems was based on a 'factory model' that aligned well with the needs of the manufacturing sector during and following the industrial revolution. It was arguably one of the great success stories in recent human history because mass education was an outcome well matched to the needs of mass production.

It's time for a new 'grand alignment'. Failure in much of school reform can be put down to lack of alignment within and between the 'internals' and 'externals'. The 'internals' are what occurs at the school in curriculum, pedagogy and the environment for learning. The 'externals' refer to the great changes that are occurring in society and the world of work. There is little point in securing alignment of the former ('internals') if there is a mismatch with what is occurring or what is needed beyond the school ('externals'). One manifestation of the problem is the current shortage of skills in the workforce – no amount of alignment among the 'internals' will assist if schools and school systems are disconnected to the 'externals', in this case the needs of society in a time of globalisation. In the larger scheme of things, this is the challenge of creating in the early years of the twenty-first century an 'education imaginary' that aligns with the 'social imaginary' (Hargreaves, 2004; Beare, 2006). Moreover, alignment extends to a limited number of 'internals', as illustrated by the fact that much of the curriculum and associated pedagogy cannot be delivered because most school buildings are obsolete, having been designed according to a model that suited the last 'grand alignment'.

The next grand alignment

There are two issues related to the next 'grand alignment' that are of particular concern. One is that the 'externals' are changing at a rapid rate and this makes long-overdue alignment in education very difficult to achieve. Expressed another way, we are still in 'catch-up' mode at a time when the world we are catching up with is changing at a rapid rate. Former Prime Minister Tony Blair outlined the nature of this change in his valedictory speech to the Labour Party conference in Manchester on 27 September 2006.

The scale of the challenges now dwarf what we faced in 1997 [when Labour was elected]. They are different, deeper, bigger, hammered out on the anvil of forces, global in nature, sweeping the world. In 1997 the challenges we faced were essentially British. Today they are essentially global. The world today is a vast reservoir of potential opportunity. New jobs in environmental technology, the creative industries, financial services. Cheap goods and travel. The internet. Advances in science and technology. In ten years we will think nothing of school-leavers going off to university anywhere in the world. But with all these opportunities comes huge insecurity . . . The British people today are reluctant global citizens. We must make them confident ones.

(Blair, 2006a)

Tony Blair made clear the impact on schools: 'The same global forces changing business are at work in public services too. New ways of treating. New ways of teaching. New technologies.'

The Blair government achieved some degree of alignment in education, moving from a one-size-fits-all approach to secondary education, which was well-suited to an era of mass production, toward a system of specialist schools, which takes account of diversity, interests, aptitudes and needs in the twenty-first century. There is realisation that much of the curriculum and many of the approaches to learning and teaching cannot be carried out in obsolete or run-down facilities. The Building Schools for the Future programme is intended to re-build or refurbish in a major way about 90 per cent of the space in secondary schools. The Blair Government took the lead in personalising learning and good progress has been made in many schools. The paradox is that personalising learning, indeed the personalising of all services, must succeed as new opportunities are pursued in an era of globalisation. This paradox will be resolved; it will not disappear with the retirement of Tony Blair. His successor as prime minister, former Chancellor Gordon Brown, affirmed this in his address at the same conference:

And we cannot leave public services as they were, we must build them around the personal aspirations of the individual. And let me say that the renewal of New Labour must and will be built upon these essential truths: a flexible economy, reformed and personalised public services, public and private sectors not at odds but working together, so that we can truly deliver opportunity and security, not just for some but for all.

(Brown, 2006)

There is recognition of the need for 'grand alignment' in Australia. Writing in *The Australian*, editor-at-large Paul Kelly stated that 'the 21st century task facing Australia is how to leverage its assets to succeed in the globalised age, and this requires a flexible economy, a highly educated workforce and a sound system of governance' (Kelly, 2006a). Two of these requirements as they concern schools are taken up in Chapter 4 ('workforce') and Chapter 5 ('governance'). Australia will have a national election in 2007 and Kelly expects that it will be 'a contest over different models to manage globalisation'. This may well be the case in elections to take place in other nations over the next five years, including the next contest in the UK.

The second issue is that, while there is broad recognition that dramatic change is needed, even a long overdue 'grand alignment', policy and practice in most settings are still 'business as usual'. In terms of the famous OECD scenarios for the future of schooling (OECD, 2001a), it is still a matter of the status quo in the form of 'bureaucratic systems continue' rather than either of the re-schooling scenarios: 'schools as focused learning organisations' or 'schools as core social centres'. There is little sense of the 'adaptive state', that is, acceptance of the idea that 'we need new systems capable of continuously reconfiguring themselves to create new sources of public value' (Bentley and Wilsdon, 2004, p. 16).

Some governments have commissioned studies on the future of schools, suggesting a commitment to re-designing current arrangements to ensure that the desired future state is achieved. Yet these same governments are still organised in basically the same way as far as education is concerned. They often respond to criticism of their efforts by offering a traditional defence based on matters such as increases in levels of funding, reductions in class size and growth in the number of teachers, when a 'new enterprise logic' is required (Caldwell, 2006).

A justified sense of frustration is evident in *Essential Questions for the Future School* (Futures Vision Group, 2006). Authors made reference to Hedley Beare's now famous description of Angelica. He invited the reader to imagine a child starting school in 2001 and the kind of world in which she will spend the rest of her life. 'Hullo. I am Angelica. I am 5 years old. I really don't have much of a past. In fact,

I am the future' (Beare, 2001). Beare framed his book around a view of how schools need to change for people like Angelica. The Futures Vision Group declared that 'If we cannot respond to Angelica today, what hope have we of responding to her five-year-old son or daughter in 2025? There is now an urgency that has characterised schooling for too long.' . . . 'We need to be outraged that we have not responded to the 2001 Angelica. If we cannot, even today, respond to her, how can we create schools for the future?'

The 'essential questions' posed by the Futures Vision Group include the following: Why is education configured in the way it is? What do we take for granted that we might question and change? How can schools justify much of what they do? Why do so many students still leave at the end of compulsory education with so little to show for it? Why do we still depend on outmoded, industrial age thinking when working with complex organisations? What are the consequences for students in meeting the challenges of the twenty-first century if we do not transform our current practice? What are the consequences for society if our students are unable to meet these challenges?

Alignment about alignment

This book is not the first in education that places the concept of alignment at centre-stage in efforts to achieve the transformation of schools. Its uniqueness lies in the extension of our earlier work on self-managing schools, the broader notion of resources that draw on four kinds of capital and the student focus in planning and budgeting. We acknowledge the contributions of others who have paved the way or are moving ahead with different but complementary intent.

Much work was done in the 1990s in the United States, in particular, on efforts to create new designs for schools. The aim was to create comprehensive, consistent and coherent approaches to school improvement, drawing on the findings of research on good practice. There were initially nine designs promoted by the New American Schools Development Corporation (see Stringfield et al., 1996). More designs were created and a study of the impact of 29 of these yielded mixed findings as far as student learning is concerned (Borman et al., 2003). In their review of these developments, Fullan, Hill and Crévola (2006, pp. 44–5) suggested five reasons for a failure to meet expectations: (1) focus on a limited range of functions in the operation of schools; (2) over-estimation of the capacity of schools; (3)

insufficient attention to teaching and learning; (4) focus on external aspects of design rather than placing the teacher and student at the centre and (5) failure to tackle the challenge of change at the system level.

These shortcomings are addressed in *Breakthrough* (Fullan et al., 2006) and we refer to their work in Chapter 4, as it concerns personalisation and professional learning, and in Chapter 9, as it concerns 'precision', that is, the gathering and utilisation on a continuous basis of data that are needed to guide the work of teachers who seek to secure success for all of their students. Dimmock also addressed these shortcomings in *Designing the Learning-Centred School* (Dimmock, 2000). He explicitly acknowledged the importance of resources and a capacity for self-management and brought an international cross-cultural perspective to the topic.

Valuable work has been done in Australia by Frank Crowther and his colleagues at the University of Southern Queensland (USQ) in the Innovative Designs for Enhancing Achievement in Schools project (IDEAS). The IDEAS model seeks alignment between schoolwide pedagogy (intellectual capital), cohesive community (social capital), strategic foundations (spiritual capital) and infrastructure design. The integrating mechanism is powerful professional support (intellectual capital). The model has been successfully implemented in Queensland through a partnership of USQ and the Department of Education. Implementation in a limited number of schools in other jurisdictions was made possible through funding from the Australian Government's Quality Teaching Programme. In Chapter 10 we describe the successful experience of an award-winning school in the Australian Capital Territory (St Monica's Parish Primary).

Alignment in action

The concept of alignment is starting to find its place in a range of educational settings. An impressive example may be found in Texas. The University of Texas System is a consortium of 'Nine Universities. Six Health Institutions. Unlimited Possibilities'. It has 185,000 students, 77,500 staff and an annual budget of US$9.6 billion. Its Board of Regents is understandably concerned to achieve alignment among its 15 entities but extends the concept of alignment to include the needs and aspirations of society in Texas and the requirements of the nation in an era of globalisation. Significantly, it works with schools and school systems to secure alignment across all sectors of education. It has an Assistant Vice-Chancellor for Educational Alignment who heads the Office of Educational System Alignment. Its Strategic Plan 2006–2015 acknowledged that:

> The twenty-first century will be an era of increasing worldwide integration and competition in science, technology, business and education. The competition for the best minds, the best work-force, and the best ideas will heighten the importance of education as a means to social and economic mobility and success.
>
> (University of Texas System, 2006)

The Office of Educational System Alignment at the University of Texas System has designed the 'Every Child, Every Advantage' initiative which is part of the Texas response to the federal No Child Left Behind Act of 2001. It provides support for teachers and students in public schools. It administers a US$7.5 million grant to enhance reading, hiring 40 reading specialists to provide deep on-site support to 550 schools in 114 school districts. It has established its own charter school. Along with two other university systems in Texas (Texas A & M University System and Texas State University System) it secured a US$3.9 million grant from Houston Endowment, a private philanthropic organisation, to enhance teacher education in 23 colleges of education around the state.

In another development in the United States, the Governor of Colorado established the Colorado Education Alignment Council in 2005 to address the problem of misalignment in a range of educational initiatives in elementary (primary), secondary and higher education. The Governor's Executive Order acknowledged progress:

> However, the development and implementation of these various sets of standards in K–12 and higher education levels were completed independently, at different times, and with little or no interagency coordination. In order to ensure expectations for student achievement are seamless across the K–16 continuum, I hereby determine that Colorado must align its various sets of secondary and post-secondary standards for student achievement.
>
> (State of Colorado, 2005)

Powerful alignment is evident in two systems of education at the top of the tables in PISA (Programme in International Student

Assessment). Finland ranks first. Alignment is strong in terms of expectations and support for schools, the status of the teaching profession, a focus on creativity and innovation and an absence of public release of school-by-school test results (Harris, J., 2006). School performance is determined largely on the basis of self-assessment with report to the National Board of Education. The results of performance reviews are provided only to the school in question. It seems that this practice fosters high levels of trust between schools and their governing bodies and there are high rates of participation in school evaluations.

Finland ranks third on the Global Creativity Index based on three factors accounting for economic growth: technology, talent and tolerance (Florida, 2005). The 12 top ranked nations are Sweden, Japan, Finland, United States, Switzerland, Denmark, Iceland, the Netherlands, Norway, Germany, Canada and Australia, ahead of the United Kingdom (15th), France (17th) and New Zealand (18th). Strength on these indicators illustrates the extent of alignment. It is another reason why closer scrutiny of education in Finland is warranted.

The second ranked system in PISA is not a nation but a province within a nation. It is Alberta in Canada. Alberta is the best performing province in Canada and comes second to Hong Kong in mathematics, second to Finland in reading, and fourth after Finland, Japan and Hong Kong in science.

> Many educators acknowledge that over the past 30 years Alberta has quietly built the finest public education system in Canada. The curriculum has been revised, stressing core subjects (English, science, mathematics), school facilities and the training of teachers have been improved, clear achievement goals have been set and a rigorous province-wide testing programme for grades 3 (aged 7–8), 6 (10–11), 9 (13–14) and 12 (16–17) has been established to ensure they are met.
>
> *(The Economist*, 2006b)

A large majority of parents are satisfied with public schools whereas, in Canada as a whole, the proportion of students in private schools has risen by 20 per cent over the last decade.

The capital city of Alberta is Edmonton, which was a pioneer in self-managing schools. It has an impressive system of needs-based funding and choice among secondary schools. There is a trend to specialist rather than standard comprehensive schools at the secondary level. Some private schools have been absorbed into the public system.

While more needs to be done, especially in education for indigenous students and raising completion rates at the secondary level, there appears to be a high degree of alignment in Alberta. Rather than British Columbia and Ontario, which have traditionally attracted attention in the literature, what has occurred in Alberta warrants closer scrutiny.

Singapore is a fine example of how alignment is essential if a nation is to survive and flourish in an era of globalisation. Addressing the National Day Rally on 21 August 2005, shortly after becoming Prime Minister, Lee Hsien Loong (son of founding Prime Minister Lee Kuan Yew) issued a challenge.

> What will Singapore be like 40 years from now? I can't tell you. Nobody can. But I can tell you it must be a totally different Singapore because if it is the same Singapore as it is today, we're dead. We will be irrelevant, marginalised, the world will be different. You may want to be the same, but you can't be the same. Therefore, we have to re-make Singapore – our economy, our education system, our mindsets, our city.
>
> (Lee, H.L., 2005)

In 2005 the Ministry of Education in Singapore released *Nurturing Every Child: Flexibility & Diversity in Singapore Schools*, a policy that called for a more varied curriculum, a focus on learning rather than teaching, the creation of specialist schools and more autonomy for schools and teachers (Ministry of Education, Singapore, 2005). Many would ask why Singapore should embark on such a change. After all, Singapore ranked first among 49 nations in each of Grade 4 and Grade 8 for both mathematics and science in the 2003 tests in the Trends in Mathematics and Science Study (TIMSS). Singapore is a nation whose chief, if not sole, resource is its human resource. It realises there is a need to 're-make the nation' and accepts that it must also 're-make the school' if it is to achieve that end. Prime Minister Lee expressed it this way in his contribution to a special edition of *Newsweek* on the theme 'The Knowledge Revolution: Why Victory will go to the Smartest Nations & Companies': 'We are remaking ourselves into a key node in the global knowledge network, securing our place under the sun' (Lee, H.L., 2006).

These intentions are remarkable, given that Singapore was only established as a nation in its own right in 1965. In 40 years it has been transformed from a struggling colony to one of the world's most successful multi-cultural nations with a thriving economy, as described by founding Prime Minister Lee Kuan Yew in *From Third World to First* (Lee, K.Y., 2000). Singapore's vision of 'Thinking Schools, Learning Nation' captured the imagination of educators around the world when it was announced by former Prime Minister Goh Chok Tong at the 7th International Conference on Thinking in June 1997 (Goh, 1997). Singapore faces the continuing challenge of securing alignment with the needs of the nation. On the basis of its track record, it is likely to succeed.

Alignment may be more difficult to achieve in nations where there are different levels of government with a major role in education. This is the case in Australia, where the constitution assigns responsibility for education to the six states and two territories. However, the federal government plays a particularly powerful role because it is the only level of government that can levy an income tax, the proceeds of which are re-distributed to the states and territories in the form of grants to which particular conditions can be attached. The federal government has used these financial powers to require the introduction of a national system of testing and reporting and, more recently, the re-introduction of history as a subject in schools. It has provided funds to improve the quality of teaching in mathematics, science and information technology. It has been highly critical of directions in school curriculum in most states and territories.

In Australia, it could be claimed that there is a higher degree of alignment of the views of the federal government with those of parents and the wider community, as reflected in public opinion polling. This is a paradox, since it is reasonable to expect that state and territory governments have a better feel of the community pulse. Interestingly, all governments in the eight jurisdictions are Labor, whereas the federal government is Liberal National Coalition. Editor-at-large at *The Australian* is Paul Kelly, cited earlier in the chapter. He presented the case for federal intervention in curriculum (Kelly, 2006b). 'How much longer to wait? For years, the federal government has proposed a series of curriculum changes. But it needs to redouble those efforts and find new mechanisms to reform school curriculum.' Kelly did not have to wait long for a response. On 6 October 2006, federal minister Julie Bishop proposed a national curriculum, drawing an immediate negative response from her counterparts in states and territories.

Alignment and abandonment

An important reason for misalignment is the failure to abandon old practices as new practices are introduced. An example is the amount of paperwork that accrues as levels of accountability increase. School leaders by and large accept the need for accountability but they resent the amount of administrative work. What needs to be abandoned is reliance on paper and much of the traditional role of the principal. Work-flow specialists are needed to streamline administration and help school leaders move as far as possible to a paperless office, at the same time providing them with more administrative support. An extraordinary example was reported to Brian Caldwell during a national series of workshops in 2006. He participated in a talk-back session in a radio programme dealing with some of the themes in *Re-imagining Educational Leadership* (Caldwell, 2006). One listener reported that the principal of a primary school had spent the best part of two days meeting the compliance requirements of keeping budgerigars in the school!

The case for abandonment has been made in powerful terms by the Futures Vision Group of the Specialist Schools and Academies Trust (Futures Vision Group, 2006). Andy Schofield, Headteacher at Varndean School in Brighton (England) identified eight key issues to be addressed, describing the levers of transformation and practices to be abandoned. For example, for school buildings and other places where learning takes place, the levers for transformation include 'Virtual learning environments, redesigned classrooms, community and home based learning, extended independent learning assignments'. Practices to be abandoned include 'Rigid learning patterns for students (e.g. 9–3, 190 days per year), provision on one site, distinction between curricular and extracurricular, traditional piecemeal homework timetables, uncomfortable plastic chairs, traditional lunch times, poor quality food, uncivilised canteens, corridors with lino and lockers, traditional unpleasant toilets' (Schofield, 2006).

There is an important qualification to make in respect to the case for alignment. It will be readily apparent to the reader. While alignment is important, it should include a capacity for creativity, innovation, exploring the boundaries and developing a new alignment. The last 'grand alignment' resulted in the nineteenth-century factory model of schooling, the major features of which are evident in today's policy and practice. There is need for new 'grand alignment' on the scale outlined in this chapter, but a capacity to challenge the status quo and seek new alignments must also be resourced and rewarded.

The way forward

A new 'grand alignment' in education is an exciting prospect. It presents challenges and creates opportunities for policymakers at every level. This chapter has demonstrated that there are sources of capital that have not been tapped to any great extent in most settings, and transformation on a scale that secures success for all students demands strength in each type of capital, with powerful alignment that can only be achieved by outstanding governance. There will always be a concern to build financial capital, but more must be done to build spiritual and social capital. The evidence is strong that the most important resource of a school or school system is intellectual capital, and bold new strategies are required to make it strong. Chapter 4 describes and illustrates the possibilities.

Chapter 4

Intellectual capital

Introduction

If outcomes alone are an indicator of the transformation of a school, then all one needs to demonstrate success are data on student achievement, given the view that a school has been transformed if there has been significant, systematic and sustained change that secures success for all of its students. These data should show the proportion of students who were deemed to have achieved success and how this proportion changed over time. This is straightforward for secondary schools in England, for example, where the current 'rolled gold' standard is the percentage of students who achieve five good passes in examinations for the GCSE. In Chapter 2 we provided data on student achievement from 1998 to 2004 at Bellfield Primary School in Australia, which provides an exemplar in transformation, with the proportion of early years' students reading with 100 per cent accuracy increasing from about 25 per cent to 100 per cent under the most challenging circumstances.

An assessment of capacity for transformation, and progress in achieving it, can be made if attention is paid to the four forms of capital in the model for alignment described in Chapter 3 and how these are acquired, sustained and made effective through good governance. While particular attention is given in Chapters 4 and 5 to three elements in the model, namely, intellectual capital, social capital and governance, it is important to note that financial capital is important to ensure the availability of funds to build intellectual capital, and that social capital is an important aspect of both intellectual capital and governance. Chapters 6 to 9 deal with financial capital, with the centre-piece being a model for student-focused planning and resource allocation.

Chapter 4 calls for a breakthrough in thinking about intellectual capital in the context of the self-managing school. We do this in several ways. The starting point is recent work by Fullan, Hill and Crévola (2006). We then describe two new approaches for schools that seek to achieve transformation by building their intellectual capital. We provide an instrument for assessing capacity in an important aspect of intellectual capital (knowledge management) and offer benchmarks from Australia and England that will assist schools to make judgements on their strength in this area.

The need for a breakthrough

We emphasised in our earlier work that providing schools with additional authority and responsibility to make decisions through a capacity for self-management may have little or no impact on learning unless there are clear, considered, comprehensive and consistent links with learning and teaching and the support of learning and teaching (see especially Caldwell and Spinks, 1998). These links will be strong if the intellectual capital of the school is strong, that is, if all who work in or for the school are at the forefront of knowledge and skill.

There is a need for new thinking about the kind of knowledge and skill that is required to achieve the transformation of schools. The engagingly titled, award-winning *Breakthrough* (Fullan et al., 2006) is a helpful starting point. The authors provide evidence of the limits to improvement under self-management by describing how gains in literacy have plateaued in England and how decentralisation of decision-making in Chicago, Milwaukee and Seattle has not led to large-scale improvement: 'They contain glimpses of what will be required, but they fail to touch deeply day-to-day classroom instruction, and to touch it in a way that will get results for all' (Fullan et al., 2006, p. 6). Drawing on the work of Richard Elmore, they distinguish between external accountability and internal accountability, noting that no amount of the former will impact learning unless the latter is also evident (p. 8). We addressed similar issues in Chapter 3 when we observed that 'Failure in much of school reform can be put down to lack of alignment within and between the "internals" and "externals"'.

Fullan, Hill and Crévola propose a system to lift the performance of schools to achieve a 'breakthrough'. There are three components: personalisation, professional learning and precision. 'The glue that binds these three is moral purpose: education for all that raises the bar as it closes the gap' (p. 16). The consistency between these components and the model for alignment and broad themes of this book are evident. Personalising learning is central – the student is the most important unit of organisation – and we place students at the heart of the enterprise, with moral purpose expressed as 'success for all students in all settings'. Professional learning is essential in the building of intellectual capital, as explained and illustrated in the pages that follow.

Of particular interest is the concept of 'precision' as it applies to the gathering and utilisation of data. There is an unprecedented level of data washing around schools and school systems, but the breakthrough will be achieved only when 'classroom instruction in which the current sporadic data collection is streamlined, analysis is automated, and individualised instruction is delivered on a daily basis in every classroom' (p. 20). The acquisition and utilisation of data along these lines is a key component of the student-focused planning model described in Chapter 8 and illustrated in Chapter 9. It is clear that the 'breakthrough' proposed by Fullan, Hill and Crévola, and transformation on the scale we propose, requires professional talent of the highest order and processes for ensuring that all who work in or for the school are always at the cutting-edge of knowledge and skill. It is to these matters that we now turn our attention.

From workforce to talent force

There are two important processes in building the intellectual capital of the school. One is identifying, selecting and rewarding the best people to do the work. The other is ensuring that all who are so employed are at – and remain at – the forefront of knowledge and skill.

Schools and school systems have usually followed a traditional workforce approach to securing staff. If transformation is to be achieved, then all who work in or for the school need to be at the forefront of knowledge and this is why the concept of 'talent force' should be adopted for schools, as it is now being applied in a growing number of enterprises in the public and private sectors. The difference between the two approaches is illustrated in Table 4.1, adapting to education a comparison proposed by Rueff and Stringer (2006). The approaches are compared on seven dimensions.

The first and second are concerned with assumptions about

Table 4.1 Comparing workforce and talent force approaches to building intellectual capital (adapted from Rueff and Stringer, 2006)

Dimensions	Workforce approach	Talent force approach
1. Availability	Supply is assured ('arrogance')	Talent is scarce ('humility')
2. Procurement	Routine and manual	Hi-tech
3. Control	Employer in control	Shared control
4. Source	Local sourcing Stable	Global sourcing Dynamic shifts
5. Performance	'Soft' measures	'Hard' measures
6. Location	Work within borders Work by locals	Dispersed work Immigrating talent
7. Strategy	Short-sighted	Strategic, compelling

availability and processes for procurement of staff. For availability (dimension 1) the workforce approach assumes that people to fill a vacancy or to be hired to initiate a particular programme or work on a project are out there waiting to be made aware of the employment opportunity. There is a touch of arrogance about this assumption, whereas a talent force approach calls for a degree of humility; the very best people are needed and it is going to take a considerable amount of work at some cost to locate and interest them in an appointment. For procurement (dimension 2) the workforce approach follows a traditional routine, that is, an advertisement is designed, applications are invited, a preliminary short list is prepared, references are sought, a final short list is determined, interviews are conducted and an appointment is made. In contrast, a talent force approach employs new technologies to attract staff. For example, rather than waiting for a vacancy to occur, the school is always searching for the best people, and will make an offer to the very best should they express an interest. Websites and search agencies might be employed. Potential employees will register with search agencies. A line in the budget of the enterprise may be committed to cover the costs of appointment and up to one year of employment, even though there may not be an immediate need for the services of a new member of staff.

A different approach to the control of staff (dimension 3) is evident if a talent force approach is used. Traditionally, the employer was in control and the employee was expected to fall in line. In a talent force approach, the initiative lies with the employee who has sought-after knowledge and skills to the extent that there will be little difficulty in the employee taking up an alternative appointment, because the search for such capacity by other enterprises is always on, and the employee is always searching for the best opportunities.

The foregoing suggests that sources of staff will be different (dimension 4). In the traditional approach, there was considerable local sourcing. In highly centralised systems, a central personnel arm of an education department advertises for staff and often makes arrangements with local higher education institutions to employ graduates who are then placed in schools. Under a more decentralised arrangement, it may be the school that advertises and works directly with these institutions. In most instances, it is local sourcing and relatively stable sources of staff are assured. With a talent force approach, the search is national or international (global sourcing), and there may be dynamic shifts in arrangements with particular institutions that have an interest in securing the best placements for their graduates.

The approaches differ in respect to performance management (dimension 5). In the traditional workforce approach, the process is usually tightly constrained, especially where a key stakeholder such as a union is resistant. Where performance management is permitted for individuals, the measures are relatively 'soft' and there may be little differentiation in judgements about performances. Incentives and rewards are not encouraged and where they exist they are usually shared. On the other hand, in a talent force approach, performance indicators are the subject of negotiation and agreement, and these may be included in contracts of employment. Measurable targets may be part of the arrangement ('hard' measures).

There is an important difference as far as location of employment is concerned (dimension 6). Traditionally, all were expected to work at the school site, which invariably limited employment to those who lived or were prepared to live locally. If the aim of a talent force approach is to secure the services of the best people, then it may be necessary for appointees to work from another location. This is made possible by advances in technology, especially those which allow free and unlimited time through on-line audio- and video-conferencing.

In the case of classroom teaching for example, it is possible for two classrooms taught by world-class teachers to be located in different hemispheres (in the same time zone).

The two approaches reflect a different strategy (dimension 7). The traditional workforce approach is relatively short-sighted, filling positions from local sources, with 'soft' measures of performance that do not address in an objective fashion the strategic priorities of the school, to the extent that these exist. On the other hand, the talent force approach involves a more-or-less continuous search for the best people to address the strategic priorities of the school, something that may call for global sourcing, with a focus on performance that connects tightly with priorities connected to transformation ('hard' measures). It is a much more strategic and compelling approach to building the intellectual capital of the school.

Compared to schools, universities have generally adopted a talent force approach, especially for senior academic appointments at the level of professor. A review of recent advertisements by universities that seek to be world-class reveals an even sharper focus on such an approach. A remarkable advertisement appeared during the 19 workshops conducted by Brian Caldwell around Australia in July and August 2006. A four-page advertisement was placed by Macquarie University in Sydney in the higher education supplement of *The Australian*. The first page featured a single statement: 'We're recruiting for the best research brains'. The second page described clusters (teams) of traditional research disciplines, renamed in rather more exciting terms: ancient cultures; cognitive science; social inclusion; animal behaviour; earth and planetary evolution; lasers and photonics; quantum information, science and security; functional proteomics and cellular networks; climate risk/ecology and evolution. A third page described in attractive terms the history and vision of the university under the heading 'so now's the time to join us'. The fourth page listed particular positions at different academic levels for which appointments were sought. It was made clear that, while appointments would be governed by an existing enterprise agreement that concluded in 2006, successful applicants would subsequently be offered the option of an Australian Workplace Agreement, which is essentially an individual contract under negotiated terms and conditions.

Why not use the same talent force approach across-the-board for schools which seek to build their intellectual capital in pursuit of transformation? Some schools are already doing it. Private, non-government, independent schools often employ a search agency to seek out the best 'talent' for senior appointment, especially at the level of principal, and negotiate terms and conditions on behalf of the governing body. One private (non-government, independent) school in Victoria has almost every element of the talent force approach listed in Table 4.1 in place. A public (government or state school) in Tasmania was seriously constrained in its attempt to locate staff in an area of shortage elsewhere in the state and in another country. The Minister for Education, Science and Training in the Australian Government has called for incentives and rewards based on performance, and a capacity for schools in challenging circumstances to have the financial capacity to attract the best teachers. However, as noted in Chapter 3, education in Australia is the responsibility of states and territories and there are few plans in place to adopt such an approach for public (government, state) schools.

In summary: 'The real value of great talent management is not on the compulsory, regulatory or compliance side. The real value comes when [schools] realise that talent management is one of the greatest [educational] opportunities over the next decade and beyond' (adapted from Rueff and Stringer, 2006).

Outsourcing for radical transformation

It was not so long ago that the idea of outsourcing some of the work traditionally reserved for permanent staff in a school or school system was anathema. It was an example of privatisation in public education. Until recently it was a practice for the private sector in non-education fields. However, with the introduction of local management of schools and removal of constraints on where support can be sourced, there are now more examples of outsourcing by schools who can select from a range of providers. We called for such an approach in *Beyond the Self-Managing School* (Caldwell and Spinks, 1998). One of 100 strategic intentions for schools and school systems was 'Schools seeking more autonomy will utilise every capacity that is made available under existing schemes of self-management, including where possible and feasible the outsourcing of services where there is a benefit to the school' (p. 218). Progress since 1998 is illustrated in a small but increasing number of state schools in England outsourcing an entire division of their operations, for example, financial management.

A more systematic approach to outsourcing is now emerging. Jane

Linder is Research Director of the Accenture Institute. She has written an engaging book on the topic under the title *Outsourcing for Radical Change: A Bold Approach to Enterprise Transformation* (Linder, 2004). She identified eight reasons for/benefits of outsourcing: access to 'top-drawer' skills and capacities, speed, 'wake-up calls', reduce costs, achieve operational visibility, build instant capacity, gain financial flexibility and secure third-party funding. She proposed four ways to outsource, depending on the stage in the life cycle of the enterprise when outsourcing has merit. With minor adaptation, these are illustrated in Figure 4.1.

Brian Caldwell observed an exemplary approach to outsourcing that had elements of each of the four approaches illustrated in Figure 4.1. The setting was the recently created Harefield Academy in England (an academy is a specialist secondary school, usually in challenging circumstances, to be re-opened in new premises with additional public funding and significant support from one or more private sponsors). The visit to the school revealed run-down buildings offering substandard facilities to staff and students. The principal and her leadership team recognised that many students had low self-esteem and did not have high expectations for what they could achieve at school. The expectations of staff for their students were also not high. There was the possibility that students and staff could move to the new setting and little might change as far as outcomes were concerned. It was decided to outsource the task of raising expectations and levels of self-esteem and to do so in less than six

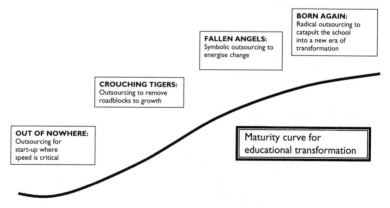

Figure 4.1 Four ways to outsource for radical transformation in schools (adapted from Linder, 2004).

months. The school secured the services of a small company that specialised in this field (Human Utopia at www.humanutopia.com). The consultants used a combination of methods. They changed the attitudes of students and staff, who worked beside the consultants and gained skills in the process.

This is a highly specialised area of work and outsourcing made sense. It fitted well with each of the four stages in the maturity curve illustrated in Figure 4.1. It was 'out of nowhere', with outsourcing to ensure rapid start-up when students and staff moved to the new facility. It was an example of the 'crouching tigers' approach, because it was outsourcing to address what was seen as a roadblock to student achievement (it is noteworthy that the public face of Accenture, a company that specialises in outsourcing, is top golfer Tiger Woods). It reflected a 'fallen angels' approach in the sense that it energised staff who could then use their newly acquired skills to maintain this aspect of the transformation. It was also a 'born again' strategy, because it helped to 'catapult the school into a new era of transformation'.

There is little doubt that a shift to a talent force approach in a global arena must and will occur. It is one of the challenges facing the public sector in education. It is consistent with the challenge presented by Tony Blair in his valedictory speech to the Labour Party in September 2006, as reported in Chapter 3. This is the context for securing alignment of intellectual capital with the needs of schools that have made a commitment to transformation.

Knowledge management

The shift from a workplace approach to a talent force approach, including outsourcing, is an example of one set of processes to build the intellectual capital of the school, namely identifying, selecting and rewarding the best people to do the work. It is also an example of another set of processes for ensuring that these people, once selected, remain at the forefront of knowledge and skill for as long as they serve the school. This takes us into the field of knowledge management.

Knowledge management in education refers to the creation, dissemination and utilisation of knowledge for the purpose of improving learning and teaching and to guide decision-making in every domain of professional practice. According to Bukowitz and Williams (1999), 'knowledge management is the process by which the organisation generates wealth from its intellectual or knowledge-based assets'. In the case of school education, knowledge management refers to the process by which a school achieves the highest levels of student learning that are possible from its intellectual or knowledge-based assets.

Schools and school systems face the challenge of creating and sustaining a powerful capacity for knowledge management if the vision of transformation is to be realised, that is, success is secured for all students in all settings. This is not simply an enhanced capacity for in-service training. It means ensuring that all teachers and others who work in or for the school are at all times at the forefront of knowledge and skill.

Schools that are exemplary in knowledge management use a range of approaches. Increasingly, consistent with the new enterprise logic of schools, they do not operate in isolation but join networks to share knowledge, address common problems and pool resources. The purpose of this section of Chapter 4 is to describe a self-assessment instrument that will assist schools to determine their current capacity for knowledge management and how they can enhance the process.

The instrument is contained in Appendix 2 as the Self-Assessment of Intellectual Capital. It is a 40-item survey adapted (with permission) for schools from one designed at Create in Tunbridge Wells in England (Rajan, 1999 as reproduced in Bahra, 2001). There are three parts to the survey: systems (14 items), values (14 items) and behaviours (12 items). Examples of 'systems' include benchmarking ('we identify and implement outstanding practice in or reported by other schools, especially those in similar circumstances, with appropriate adaptation to suit our setting') and communities of practice ('we encourage self-organised groups in which staff exchange ideas on common issues, practices, problems and possibilities'). Examples of 'values' include recognition ('we praise individuals for exemplary work in knowledge management') and immediate feedback ('we ensure that staff receive immediate feedback on their work'). Examples of 'behaviours' include absence of jargon ('we avoid ambiguous, meaningless terms which cause confusion and irritation') and benefits ('we demonstrate that the sharing of professional knowledge results in a reduction in the intensity of work').

Completing the instrument was one activity in workshops conducted in England in April 2006, organised by the Specialist Schools and Academies Trust (SSAT), and in Australia in July and August

2006, organised by the Australian College of Educators. Those in England were conducted in Birmingham, Darlington, London and Manchester. There were 19 workshops in Australia conducted in the capital cities and at least one regional centre in every state (New South Wales, Queensland, South Australia, Tasmania, Victoria and Western Australia) and territory (Australian Capital Territory and Northern Territory). Table 4.2 contains the low and high scores as well as the mean scores, expressed as a percentage in each instance.

For each country, the average number of responses at each workshop was about 20 (not all participants completed the survey; school teams often completed the survey as a group). For England, the mean of the 78 responses was 62.8, with a low of 40 and a high of 84. The lowest and highest means among the four workshops were 59.4 and 68.6, respectively. For Australia, the mean of the 400 responses was 58.4, with a low of 20 and a high of 84. The lowest and highest means among the 19 workshops were 48.7 and 66.9, respectively.

It is not appropriate to report responses on a location-by-location basis since those attending could not be considered a representative sample of leaders for each location. It is reasonable to regard the overall mean scores, as reported in Table 4.2, as representative for each country, subject to two qualifications. First, participants were pre-disposed to professional development (an important aspect of knowledge management) since they chose to register for the workshops. Second, all participants in England were from secondary schools whereas, in Australia, while a large majority were from schools, there was representation from primary and secondary schools and there were significant numbers from district or regional offices, universities and technical and further education institutes. Subject to these qualifications, it might be surmised that the higher mean score for England reflects the relatively greater attention to professional development of leaders and networking in schools than is currently the case in Australia. The wider range of scores in Australia is

Table 4.2 Benchmarks for knowledge management based on self-assessments in workshops in Australia and England

Country	Workshops	Responses	Low (%)	High (%)	Mean (%)
England	4	78	40	84	62.8
Australia	19	400	20	97	58.4

noteworthy, with the low of 20 being obtained when one participant assigned each of the 40 items the lowest rating of 1 on the five-point scale, and the high of 97 from a participant who scored 5 for virtually all items.

Apart from its use in workshops, the self-assessment survey is useful as an analytical tool in the school setting, and readers may wish to conduct the survey among members of leadership teams or, indeed, among all staff. The benchmarks in Table 4.2 might be a helpful guide to the interpretation of results. Like all instruments of this kind, the real value comes from group discussion of the ratings for various items and consideration of whether action is required and what that action ought to be. A number of school teams attended the workshops in Australia and England and members either completed the instrument individually and then compared and discussed responses, or they considered each item together as a group and reached a consensus on what the rating ought to be. The questions are posed in terms that suggest strategies to improve performance in knowledge management. Successful implementation will help build the intellectual capital of the school.

The way forward

This chapter arguably presents greater challenges than any other as far as change to the status quo is concerned. The shift in thinking from a workforce to a talent force approach has many implications for attracting, preparing, assessing, rewarding and sustaining the top class professional. The notion that 'talent is scarce' means that additional financial resources may be needed to attract the best people, especially in difficult-to-staff locations or areas of learning. Retaining the best requires a readiness to reward outstanding performance, and this challenges some powerful interests that argue that traditional approaches to advances in the profession are sufficient, or that it is too hard or too divisive to create such schemes. Similar inertia may be encountered in outsourcing to secure expert support when it is required. The case for the status quo is often argued on the basis that outsourcing will lead to the breakdown or the privatisation of the profession. An illustration was provided of how the opposite is the case. Indeed, strategic outsourcing of support can strengthen the profession or even prevent its meltdown. Every school must build a capacity for knowledge management to ensure that all are at the forefront of knowledge. While the evidence points to intellectual capital as the most important if the aim is to secure success for all students, schools and school systems need to come to terms with the often neglected field of social capital. Aligning each of the four forms of capital requires outstanding governance. These matters are taken up in Chapter 5.

Chapter 5

Governance and social capital

Introduction

The concept of governance is finding its way into the lexicon of leaders and managers in education. Some observers are sceptical. It sounds as if those who use it are adopting a new form of jargon when they should be referring to government, or they are endeavouring to elevate what is essentially a straightforward approach to decision-making by the governing body of the school. Such scepticism is ill-founded because governance is precisely the right term to describe what is essential if schools in the century are to be transformed. It is an especially important concept in achieving alignment. Chapter 5 defines governance, explains the connections to social capital and financial capital, makes clear that good governance is necessary in alignment, and describes an instrument for self-assessment of a capacity for good governance and another that focuses on the acquisition and allocation of resources. The chapter concludes with a set of 'enduring principles', complementing 'first principles' (Chapter 1) and 'core principles' (Chapter 2).

What is governance?

A definition of governance and a framework for assessment of its practice were the starting points in a project of the Human Resource Development Working Group of Asia Pacific Economic Cooperation (APEC) on *Best Practice Governance: Education Policy and Service Delivery* (Department of Education, Science and Training, 2005). The following is based on a definition of governance provided by the Governance Working Group of the International Institute of Administrative Sciences (1996).

- Governance refers to the process whereby elements in a society wield power and authority, and influence and enact policies and decisions concerning public life and economic and social development.
- Governance is a broader notion than government, whose principal elements include the constitution, legislature, executive and judiciary. Governance involves interaction between these formal institutions and those of civil society.

This definition suggests that descriptions of governance should include but go beyond accounts of how policies are determined and decisions are made, and by which institutions. The notion that governance is concerned with the interaction between these and civil society suggests a broader approach. Civil society is considered here to be the network of mutually supporting relationships between government, business and industry, education and other public and private sector services, community, home and voluntary agencies and institutions.

The applicability of the concept to schools is readily apparent if one takes account of the extent to which links with civil society have been made in successful schools in recent years. In the past, most schools had few connections; they were, to a large extent, stand-alone institutions. It is for this reason that governing bodies did not concern themselves with notions of governance because they could get by with relatively closed approaches to decision-making. The reader will readily see a connection between the links with civil society and the notion of social capital. This connection is considered in more detail at this point.

Social capital and civil society

There is growing recognition of the importance of social capital, both generally and in relation to education. It was not until 2006 that the Australian Bureau of Statistics (ABS) released its first report on indicators of social capital, which it conceived 'as being a resource available to individuals and communities founded on networks of mutual support, reciprocity and trust'. This view aligns with that adopted in our book: social capital provides a pool of resources that can be employed to support schools. The report refers to research on 'the benefits of social capital for individual outcomes in areas such as health, education, employment and family wellbeing and also in fostering community strength and resilience' (ABS, 2006, p. vi).

The OECD defines social capital as 'networks, together with shared norms, values and understandings that facilitate cooperation within and among groups' (OECD, 2001b cited in ABS, 2006, p. vi). For our purposes we consider social capital to refer to the strength of formal and informal partnerships and networks involving the school, parents, community, business and industry, indeed, all individuals, agencies, organisations and institutions that have the potential to support and, where appropriate, be supported by the school.

One can get a sense of the strength of the social capital of a school by addressing six questions, listed below. The first invites the reader to map the connections between the school and other entities. The second considers networking arrangements to be an important aspect of social capital. The third acknowledges that the other entity in the partnership must also gain from the arrangement, otherwise the partnership will not be sustained. The fourth acknowledges that leadership and resources are required for building social capital. The fifth, related to the fourth, calls for a commitment on the part of a school system to support schools in their efforts to build social capital. The sixth deals with a particular way in which social capital can be built, namely, co-locating the school with other services.

1 Which individuals, organisations, agencies and institutions in the public and private sectors, in education and other fields, including business and industry, philanthropy and social entrepreneurship, would be included in a mapping of current partnerships that support the school?

2 Does the school draw from and contribute to networks to share knowledge, address problems and pool resources?

3 Have partnerships been developed to the extent that each entity gains from the arrangement? Does the school assist each of its partners to measure outcomes, achieve transparency, improve accountability and gain recognition for its efforts? Are partnerships sustained?

4 Is there leadership of these efforts in the school? Have resources been committed and have roles and responsibilities been determined where leadership is distributed?

5 Do the school and the networks of which it is a part receive support at the system level to assist in efforts to build social capital? Is there appreciation at the central level that it ('the

centre' or its dispersed regional or district offices) is but one of several agencies of support for schools and networks of schools, and that its chief role in the years ahead is to ensure that this support is of the highest standard?

6   Is the school co-located with other services in the community and are these services utilised in support of the school? Such services include health, sport, arts, knowledge, health, welfare, law and religious. If co-location does not exist, have plans been made at the system level for initiatives in the future that reflect a whole-of-government or whole-of-community approach?

These questions were posed in four workshops in England in April 2006 and the 19 workshops conducted throughout Australia in July and August 2006. In each instance participants prepared a map of partnerships between the school and other entities, as invited in Question 1. The maps were complex. Most participants agreed they were far more complex than they would have been if drawn three years ago and they expect they will become even more complex in the next three years.

Good governance is necessary for successful alignment

This complexity is the reason why governance, as defined earlier, is so important if alignment is to be achieved. The processes of developing policies, setting priorities, preparing plans and budgets, building partnerships to support the effort, making decisions on the basis of good data and being transparent throughout, are far more demanding than ever before. The four kinds of capital must work together in a coherent and consistent manner. This is why governance in a school is just as complex as governance in other fields of public and private endeavour.

What a contrast to the days when there were few if any partnerships with other entities, no delegated budgets, staff were assigned to schools by a central authority, schools were largely data-free environments, and there were few demands to ensure success for all students in all settings. Governance was not an important consideration under these conditions. Leadership in the classic heroic tradition was valued, as was running a tight ship, but most decision-making was routine.

There are important implications for governing bodies. The Department for Education and Skills in England publishes *A Guide to the Law for School Governors* (DfES, 2006). The following points summarise the status and powers of governing bodies, as adapted from the indicated sections of the guide:

- The governing bodies of community, community special and maintained nursery schools are corporate bodies (3–1) (Chapter 3 Paragraph 1).
- The governing bodies of foundation, foundation special, voluntary controlled and voluntary aided schools are corporate bodies with exempt charitable status (3–2).
- Because it is a corporate body, individual governors are generally protected from personal liability as a result of the governing body's decisions and actions (3–4).
- At a school with a delegated budget, the governing body has general responsibility for the conduct of the school with a view to promoting high standards of educational achievement (3–7).
- The governing body must exercise its functions with a view to fulfilling a largely strategic role in the running of the school. It should establish the strategic framework by setting aims and objectives for the school, adopting policies for achieving those aims and objectives and setting targets for achieving those aims and objectives (3–18).
- The headteacher has responsibility for the internal organisation, management and control of the school and for the implementation of the strategic framework established by the governing body (3–20).
- The governing body is responsible to the local education authority for the way a school is run (3–24).
- Governing bodies are required to set and publish targets for their pupils' performance in Key Stage 2 and 3 on national curriculum tests and in public examinations at 15 (3–26).
- The governing body as a whole should take out insurance to cover its potential liability for negligence in carrying out its responsibilities. Cover must now be regarded as essential. Although legal action against teachers and schools for breaches of professional duty is still rare, claims (for example for 'failure to educate') are becoming more frequent (3–37). Personal claims against school governors are very rare indeed (3–38).
- Maintained schools are able to federate under one governing body (21–1). A federation shall not contain more than five schools (21–2). More informal collaborative arrangements

between maintained schools and non-maintained schools such as academies and independent schools are possible, but these may not include federation of the governing bodies or formal joint committees of the governing bodies (21–3).

Governing bodies are required to adopt an instrument of government that complies with constitutional regulations that came into force in 2003. The new education bill that provides for schools to acquire a trust, employ their own staff and manage their own assets has major implications for governing bodies that choose to take up the new arrangements.

While these matters are the subject of separate legislation, it is evident that issues of corporate governance are very similar to those of directors of corporations. Leblanc and Gillies (2005) drew on studies of for-profit companies in the private sector, government-owned enterprises and not-for-profit organisations, and concluded that, despite increased attention to governance in the 1990s, there is 'very little knowledge about the relationship of corporate governance to corporate performance, and almost no knowledge about how boards actually work' (Leblanc and Gillies, 2005, p. 1). They acknowledge that, in research to date, 'an explanation of how boards make decisions is missing although this may well be the most important factor in determining the effectiveness of the governance of an enterprise' (p. 25).

A model of good governance and powerful alignment

New approaches to governance in England are especially noteworthy in the case of federations, that is, in formal partnerships between schools that are intended to deliver benefits to participants. Foremost among these are benefits in the way resources are acquired and allocated. An example is the Haberdashers' Aske's Federation in South London that comprises two academies. One is Haberdashers' Aske's Hatcham College, which has a long association with the Haberdashers' Livery Company that has supported education for more than 300 years, and the Knights Academy, formerly the Malory School. They offer specialisms in music and sport, respectively, operating as separate 11–18 (age of students) schools with separate delegated budgets from the federation but with a shared sixth form. The federation was formed in 2005.

There is frank and open acknowledgement that this is a federation of the strong and the weak. Hatcham had 1,384 students in 2006, with 94 per cent achieving five good passes in GCSE in that year, up from 73 per cent in 2001. Free school meals (FSM) are provided to 18 per cent of students, 15 per cent of whom have English as a second language (ESL). It was judged to be an 'excellent school' in an Ofsted inspection in 2003. In contrast, Knights Academy has 750 students, with just 9 per cent of students achieving five good passes in GCSE in 2005, rising to 29 per cent in 2006, one year after federation. At Knights, 52 per cent of students receive FSM and 20 per cent are ESL students. There is a single admissions process, with no more than 10 per cent of students selected by aptitude in the two areas of specialism.

Dr Elizabeth Sidwell is the Chief Executive Officer, that is, the senior educational leader serving both schools. She describes the relationship between the two schools in the following terms: 'This is our federation: the very strong and the very weak. Together, we are raising the bar and narrowing the gap. Both schools now thrive and both will be strong. It's all about having a vision and sticking with it.' That vision 'is one where all students are inspired to reach their full potential, no matter their ability or background'. Improvement at Knights in 'narrowing the gap' in just one year is impressive.

The federation has a single governing body whose role and that of the Chief Executive Officer are clearly defined in a formal statement. 'The governors' role is comparable to that of non-executive directors. The Chairman's role is that of a non-executive chairman of a company, but of necessity he is required to have a close working relationship with the Chief Executive, who will in particular circumstances need to refer to him for ad hoc decisions or endorsements in respect of matters of urgency which arise. These may require action between governors' meetings, but their nature is not such as to necessitate a special meeting of the board of governors.

> Fundamentally, the main role of the governors is, in close consultation with the Chief Executive, Chief Financial Officer and the principals of Hatcham and Knights, the formulation of policy and strategy for federation. Governors do not take direct responsibility for the implementation of policy, although they do have a role in the monitoring of targets (as outlined in the Development Plans) and achievements. The governors are accountable to students, to parents and to the local community

as well as to sponsors, for the overall performance of the Federation.

(Haberdashers' Aske's Federation, 2005, p. 1)

The governing body has three committees: Finance, Premises and General Purposes; Standards; and Liaison. Each of the constituent schools has its own principals and staffing arrangements. There are two deputy principals with federation-wide responsibilities, including information technology, timetabling and assessment for learning. They operate at principal level.

Dr Sidwell described her role in the text of a speech provided to the authors.

> I am not a head any more. I am a CEO. Some of you may flinch at the corporate language. But what other title will do? My bursar is a CFO. My job is largely strategic but I still do assemblies – fewer – and lesson observations.

> I administer two schools over three sites, and am in negotiations for two primary schools to complete the set. Without the primaries, I already lead over three hundred staff and two and half thousand children. I work as a consultant to other academies in transition. I also head a successful teacher training consortium of ten schools, both state and independent. The federation's annual budget puts us in the top ten per cent of all charities in the country. This is a new level of responsibility.

It is clear that, in these roles, Dr Sidwell is an example of a 'system leader', as that role is emerging in England. She considers the federation to have a number of benefits, as summarised in these excerpts from a presentation:

> A federation can offer both economies of scale and the advantages of scale – I can retain senior managers within the federation who would normally have to range from school to school for the right promotions. I don't lose them but rather see them develop: deputy principals to principals, site managers to facilities managers. My Chief Financial Officer is of a quality that the budget of a single school could not afford. Most of all, a federation gives a head who has reached the top and still looks upward a further, final challenge: one that can expand to the limit of your vision. Working within a team – everything is made possible.

A federation is a way of becoming much bigger without losing the personal scale at each school. It disseminates best practice quickly between sites that still have enough autonomy to innovate and experiment.

Federations are about the long term. Bound together in law. Schools with informal ties can be fair weather friends, but when the pressure drops, there is no reason for them to stand by you in the storm. Sustainable even after I go! A federation is bound together for better or worse: that incentive commits us all to seek the best for the future. A federation recognises that a school is strongest in partnership with other schools.

There are several categories of 'executive heads' in England. Some take on responsibility for schools in difficulties while remaining heads of their own schools. There is no formal federation in these circumstances. Dr Sidwell sees particular advantages in a federation. 'I have seen super heads brought in and ground down by schools in my area. They were expected to do it all on their own. A federation of the strong and the weak gives a firm shoulder for a school in difficulties to lean on as it pushes itself upwards.'

Dr Sidwell agreed to comment on how the different forms of capital set out in Chapter 3 are aligned at the Haberdashers' Aske's Federation. As far as intellectual capital is concerned, she highlighted the manner in which the federation can retain its most experienced and skilled staff and referred to the way in which the federation 'inspires staff to greater heights and levels of involvement'. She described how a long-serving head of department in one school was challenged and extended in ways not possible in the past because he could take up a key post across the federation. The financial capital of the two schools is made more effective in a federation, with economies of scale in areas like ICT and reprographics, and 'pump priming' when the income from the sixth form enrolments in the stronger school could be used to stimulate enrolments in the other. There is one overall income stream but there are two budgets, one for each school, but virement (transferability) across each budget is used to good effect. Spiritual capital is manifested in the values that have been embraced, with a focus on Haberdashers' motto of 'Serve and Obey' and the embedding of 'respect and responsibility' in the Haberdashers brand. The federation has close links with the community and is an active participant in several networks (social capital). It is a two-way arrangement, with the federation gaining from and contributing to others. It coordinates primary and secondary sporting activities in the Lewisham borough and is the lead school in an initial teacher education consortium of ten secondary schools.

The shared culture is enhanced in a range of ways. Students in the two schools are linked by membership of houses that span both schools. The uniform is the same and there is a shared curriculum, learning ethos and pedagogy. Staff in different learning areas in the two schools meet together, identifying their respective strengths and priorities for development. Each provides support to the other, with cross-school visits, observations, joint ventures and 'job swaps'.

Assessing a school's capacity for good governance

The World Bank Group (2001) proposed a range of indicators for governance, noting that 'new global standards of governance are emerging' and that 'citizens . . . are demanding better performance on the part of their governments'. Appendix 3 contains an instrument that provides a Self-Assessment of Governance. It is adapted from the work in the APEC (Asia Pacific Economic Cooperation) project (DEST, 2005) that drew on the work of the International Institute of Administrative Sciences (1996) and the World Bank Group (2001).

There are five domains for assessment: purpose, process, policy, scope and standards. Each domain has one or more elements, each with one or more indicators. 'Purpose' is linked to outcomes, with the indicator being 'There is a clearly stated connection between the mission of the school and intended outcomes for students'. This should be understood in a larger frame, that is, outcomes should reflect the needs and expectations of society as well as the aspirations of students, bearing in mind that the school seeks to secure success for all students. The second domain is 'process' as it concerns the engagement of stakeholders. The indicator is 'Policies and plans have been prepared after consultation with key stakeholders within the school and the wider community'. The remaining domains with associated elements are 'policy' (legitimacy, representativeness, accountability and efficiency), 'scope' (financial capital, intellectual capital, social capital) and 'standards' (specificity, data, transparency, replication and ownership). There are 20 indicators and those completing the instrument rate each on a scale from 1 (low) to 5 (high). The total of ratings is therefore a score out of 100.

The instrument was adapted for use in four workshops conducted in England in April 2006. Several items were re-worded on these occasions to focus specifically on resources. Table 5.1 summarises the responses and these may be considered benchmarks for secondary schools in England on governance as it concerns resources. Tony Barnes, principal of Park High School in Harrow completed the instrument, as it appears in Appendix 3, subsequent to another workshop in December 2006. Governance at Park High was rated as 'Outstanding' in an Ofsted inspection in March 2006. Tony's rating of governance at his school was 81, well above the mean of 62.7 in Table 5.1 and very close to the top of the range of ratings in the four workshops. Park High is one of five schools included in Chapter 10 (Studies of Success).

The same qualifications noted in Chapter 4 in respect to the survey on knowledge management apply here. It is noteworthy that scores were spread widely, for each domain and for the total. The overall mean was 62.7 with scores ranging from 37 to 86 among the 78 individuals or groups that participated in the self-assessment.

The instrument is recommended as a tool for analysis in the school setting, either in its general form as contained in Appendix 3, or with adaptation to deal with a specific aspect of governance, as was done for the workshops in England.

The acquisition and allocation of resources

A major responsibility of those with a role in governance is the acquisition and allocation of resources. Governing bodies and school councils normally have responsibility for approving a budget and monitoring its implementation. Consistent with the approach in

Table 5.1 Benchmarks for governance based on self-assessments in workshops in England (78 responses in 4 workshops)

Domain (out of)	Purpose (5)	Process (5)	Policy (20)	Scope (15)	Standards (55)	Total (100)
Mean	3.4	2.9	12.8	9.7	34.1	62.7
Range	2–5	1–5	5–18	3–14	19–51	37–86

this book, resources are defined broadly and the notion of capital is preferred, so this aspect of governance is concerned with the forms of capital considered in Chapter 3 and the importance of aligning them.

The first task is to update a list of indicators for effective resource allocation in schools. The authors' first book contained a model for self-managing schools that proved helpful in several countries (Caldwell and Spinks, 1988). The foundation of this work lay in a Project of National Significance in Australia, known as the Effective Resource Allocation in Schools Project (ERASP). Indicators for effective resource allocation were drawn from the literature of the time and schools that satisfied the criteria were selected for further study. The outcome was a model for self-management.

These indicators are contained in Table 5.2. They reflect a constrained view of resources, because the focus was on money and the

Table 5.2 A constrained view of effective resource allocation in schools

Domain	Characteristic
Process	There is a systematic and identifiable process in which:

1. Educational needs are determined and placed in an order of priority.
2. Financial resources are allocated according to priorities among educational needs.
3. There is opportunity for appropriate involvement of staff, students and the community.
4. Participants are satisfied with their involvement in the process.
5. Consideration is given to evaluating the impact of resource allocation.
6. A budget document is produced for staff and others which outlines the financial plan in understandable fashion.
7. Appropriate accounting procedures are established to monitor and control expenditure.
8. Money can be transferred from one category of the budget to another as needs change or emerge during the period covered by the budget.

(Continued overleaf)

Table 5.2 Continued

Domain	Characteristic
Outcomes	1. High priority educational goals are consistently satisfied through the planned allocation of resources of all kinds. 2. Actual expenditure matches intended expenditure, allowing for flexibility to meet emerging and/or changing needs. 3. There is general understanding and broad acceptance of the outcomes of budgeting.

(Caldwell and Spinks, 1988)

preparation of an annual budget. It sufficed at the time and, in most respects, it is still a worthwhile guide for the preparation and implementation of a one-year budget. However, times have changed, and the annual budget is just one of several plans that should be framed by a multi-year development plan for the school. Moreover, money is now recognised as just one resource to support the transformation of the school.

Table 5.3 offers a contemporary view of effective resource allocation in schools that includes a broader view of resource. For example,

Table 5.3 A contemporary view of indicators of effective resource allocation

Domain	Characteristic
Process	There is a systematic and identifiable process in which: 1. Annual planning occurs in the context of a multi-year development plan for the school. 2. Educational needs are determined and placed in an order of priority on the basis of data on student achievement, evidence-based practice and targets to be achieved. 3. Resources to be acquired and allocated include intellectual and social capital. 4. A range of sources are included in plans for the acquisition and allocation of resources, including

(Continued overleaf)

Table 5.3 Continued

Domain	Characteristic
	money allocated by formula from the school system, funds generated from other sources, other kinds of support from public and private organisations and institutions, and resources shared for the common good in networks or federations. 5. There is appropriate involvement of all stakeholders in the planning process, including representatives of sources of support. 6. The financial plan has a multi-year outlook as well as an annual budget, with all components set out in a manner that can be understood by all stakeholders. 7. Appropriate accounting procedures are established to monitor and control expenditure. 8. Money can be transferred from one category of the budget to another as needs change or emerge during the period covered by the budget. 9. Plans for knowledge management and the building of social capital, including philanthropy and the contributions of social entrepreneurs, are included in or complement the financial plan. 10. All plans specify how processes and outcomes are to be evaluated.
Outcomes	1. Targets are consistently achieved through the planned allocation of resources of all kinds. 2. Actual expenditure matches intended expenditure, allowing for flexibility to meet emerging and/or changing needs. 3. There is general understanding and broad acceptance of the outcomes of resource acquisition and allocation.

intellectual and social capital are included. Money allocated to the school by formula in a 'global budget' or 'resource package' is just one source of resource, albeit the largest in most schools in systems of public education. Multi-year outlooks are included. There is recognition of the importance of data and an evidence-base, together with targets. The budget is just one of several plans. There should also be plans for knowledge management and the building of social capital, including philanthropy and the contributions of social entrepreneurs. It is proposed that indicators in Table 5.3 be adopted in schools.

A self-assessment based on a contemporary view of resources, as reflected in the indicators in Table 5.3, is contained in Appendix 4 as the Self-Assessment of Resources. It can be completed in similar fashion to Self-Assessment of Intellectual Capital (Appendix 2) and Self-Assessment of Governance (Appendix 3). A five-point scale is provided for each item, ranging from 1 (low) to 5 (high). There are two parts (domains) in the instrument, one dealing with processes (ten items) and the other with outcomes (two items). These should be considered separately, for a total out of 50 for process and out of 10 for outcomes. Outcomes are, of course, the over-riding consideration. The instrument is a useful starting point for analysis and subsequent planning by the governing body or school council, or by leadership and management teams in the school.

Enduring principles

1   Governing bodies should operate to the highest standards of corporate governance. Priority should be placed on, and resources committed to, the assessment and development of capacity to achieve them.
2   Leaders and managers in schools should operate to the highest standards of practice in acquiring, allocating and utilising resources. Such practice should be student focused, data-driven, evidence-based and targeted-oriented. Priority should be placed on, and resources committed to, the assessment and development of capacity to achieve these standards.
3   Clarity and consensus is required in establishing complementary roles and responsibilities for governing bodies and principals.
4   Consistent with the contemporary view of transformation and its focus on personalising learning, the student should be the most important unit of analysis in all matters related to governance and the acquisition, allocation and utilisation of resources.
5   While legal action is likely to increase with the focus on personalising learning, it will be pre-empted to the extent that the highest standards of governance and practice in the management of resources are achieved.

Chapter 6

The funding of high quality and high equity

Introduction

Educational reforms are invariably expressed in monetary terms, both in relation to the drivers – the inputs, and to a lesser extent, the benefits to be derived from them – the outputs. This reflects the perception, if not the reality, that the allocation of money is a fundamental consideration in the pursuit of the transformation of schools. We take the view that financial capital is critical, because money is needed to build intellectual capital and financial capital can be enhanced if social capital is strong.

The starting point of this chapter is the identification of critical issues in the funding of schools at a time when efforts are being made to secure success for all students in all settings. Developments in Australia and the United Kingdom are explored. The concepts of 'high quality' and 'high equity' are introduced, firstly from an international perspective, based on work in the OECD (Organisation for Economic Cooperation and Development). Drawing on data from PISA, the strength of the relationship between student achievement and social background has been determined, enabling countries to be classified as either 'high' or 'low' as far as quality and equity are concerned. Australia and the United Kingdom are two countries that are 'high quality' and 'low equity'. A purpose of this book is to provide guidelines on how these countries can move to 'high quality' and 'high equity'. Chapter 6 provides the foundation for Chapter 7, that proposes 'next practice' in allocating funds from the centre to schools in systems of self-managing schools, and Chapters 8 and 9, that describe and illustrate a student-focused planning model to guide the allocation of funds at the school level.

Critical issues

Financial resources must be sufficient to enable schools to meet expectations. The level of funding is a vexed issue. It is common to make comparisons of educational expenditure and learning outcomes between countries and between educational systems within countries. This practice may be of value, but so often variance in expenditure is a function of cultural and industrial issues rather than issues related to student achievement. This has become evident in our recent research to find evidence on which to base the design and development of funding models for different educational jurisdictions. We find it more useful to identify the level of resources within a system by identification of 'next practice' schools that are also 'efficient' in the deployment of financial resources in efforts to personalise learning and secure success for all students. Consistent with the model for alignment set out in Chapter 3, we invariably find that these schools are also at the forefront of developing and deploying intellectual, social and spiritual capital.

In summary, our exploration of the importance of financial capital in educational transformation centres around three key issues:

* identification of the level of resources necessary for success;
* allocation of resources to schools to match the number, nature and needs of students to ensure expectations can be met, especially under challenging circumstances;
* enhancing the capacity of schools to deploy available resources to effectively and efficiently support the personalisation of learning.

Developments in Australia and the United Kingdom

We give particular attention in this and subsequent chapters to current efforts to transform education in Australia and the United Kingdom, with particular attention to Victoria and England. In both cases, educational reforms of the last decade have been driven by an unrelenting focus on learning outcomes. This focus continues to intensify. It will be the key driver of reform for the next decade and beyond.

Research continues to highlight the increased life chances for students successfully completing Year 12, in comparison with their peers who either disengage from secondary education prior to Year 12 or who fail to reach a recognised standard if they reach that point.

The *On Track* survey by the Department for Education and Training in Victoria found that 'students who leave school without completing Year 12 are four times more likely to be unemployed two years later compared with those who finish school' (*The Age*, December 28, 2005).

In the Australian states of Victoria and South Australia, the unrelenting pursuit of learning outcomes is encapsulated in a shared statement that '90 per cent of students will successfully complete Year 12 or its equivalent'. This target was established by the Bracks Labor government on winning office in Victoria in 1999 and reiterated in *The Blueprint for Government Schools* (Department for Education and Training, 2003). This target has subsequently been expanded to encompass 'all students achieving improved outcomes and the diminution of the disparity in achievement between students'. In essence this expansion is based on the view that it is unacceptable for a significant proportion of students to fail. Reducing disparity in student achievement has significant consequences for educational reform in Victoria and elsewhere.

In England, education reform is driven by the need for 'all pupils to perform to the maximum of their potential'. Initially this resulted in a tendency to focus improvement on those students predicted to perform just below the level of five good passes (A*–C) in the GCSE. However, increasing attention is now being given to those pupils most at risk. In a speech about 'Education Improvement Partnerships' on 3 November 2005, Jacqui Smith, Minister of State for Schools, emphasised that 'one of our most ambitious targets over the next ten years is to increase the number of 16 year olds participating in learning from 75 per cent to 90 per cent' (Smith, 2005).

In essence, education reform in the UK and Australia seeks not only to improve the learning outcomes for all students but also to ensure that our most vulnerable children receive appropriate support and can take their place as successful participants in society to the common good.

As illustrated by *The Blueprint for Government Schools* (DET, 2003) in Victoria and the *Five Year Strategy for Children and Learners* (DfES, 2004a) in England, educational reform is a high priority and is being vigorously pursued through a comprehensive range of strategies encompassing all factors known to drive school improvement. These include quality of teaching, relevant curriculum, flexible pedagogies, effective leadership, appropriate infrastructure, high levels of public trust and, of course, resources that enable these to be achieved.

There is now realisation that the transformation of educa-tion requires personalisation of learning to a degree never before attempted, if all students are to remain effectively and successfully engaged until at least the end of Year 12. This personalisation is especially important for those students who are currently being failed by their respective educational systems. This position was adopted by Ruth Kelly, former Secretary of State for Education and Skills, when she gave the Ninth Specialist School Trust Annual Lecture in July, 2005:

> At the heart of our drive for school improvement is a moral imperative: a drive for social justice; a conviction that every child – wherever they come from and whatever their circum-stances – deserves a good education and the chance to realise their potential; a rock solid belief that all children can achieve.
>
> (Kelly, 2005)

It is this 'rock solid belief that all children can achieve' that is central to the purpose of this book. It is recognised that the level of resourcing to schools must address not only core learning but also those impediments to learning that are experienced by our most vulnerable students.

This commitment has remained central to the Labour Government in the UK since it was first elected in 1997, as emphasised by former Prime Minister Blair in his address to the 14th National Conference of the Specialist Schools and Academies Trust in November 2006:

> Education is the most precious gift a society can bestow on its children. When I said the top three priorities of the Government in 1997 would be education, education, education I knew then that changing educational opportunity was the surest way to changing lives, to social justice. I'm as certain of that today as I was ten years ago when I said it.
>
> (Blair, 2006b)

It is helpful to explore the resourcing of schools in England and Victoria. Not only do they share a common background in pursuing educational transformation, but they have also devolved most of the financial resources directly to schools, with provision for flexible deployment at the local level. School self-management or local management of schools has been a strong feature in these state (government) school systems since 1988 in the case of England, developing since 1994 in Victoria, so that both are now among the most devolved systems in the world.

It is intended to explore outstanding practice in these two systems in allocating resources to schools in a manner consistent with expectations for learning and the nature, needs, aptitudes and aspirations of students. It is also intended to explore outstanding practice in schools deploying these resources through effective student-focused planning. An unrelenting focus on learning outcomes may be driving educational reform but, for success to be significant, systematic and sustained, there needs to be a high level of student-focused resourcing and student-focused planning. Achievement of this congruence may well be 'next practice'.

High quality and high equity

The concepts of 'high quality' and 'high equity' are introduced at this point. These are not clichés but well-designed, evidence-based terms with international currency that are helpful in framing efforts to allocate resources to schools and within schools. The international context is established with reference to work at the OECD. Related developments are explored, with particular reference to Victoria, Australia.

Work at the OECD has illuminated the issue of the relationship between educational achievement and the socio-economic background of students by drawing on the findings of its Programme in International Student Assessment (PISA). Former Director for Education at the OECD Barry McGaw has provided a comprehensive analysis (McGaw, 2006) from which the following explanations are drawn (see also the PISA website at www.pisa.oecd.org).

Participating countries were classified according to 'quality' and 'equity'. 'Quality' is measured by the performance of 15-year olds in the PISA tests. 'Equity' is indicated by the strength of the relationship between students' achievements and their socio-economic background, information about which was also gathered in PISA. While there is an overall positive relationship between the two, disadvantaged background is not necessarily related to poor performance. For example, in Finland and Korea, social background is less substantially related to educational achievement than among participating countries taken as a whole, whereas in Australia, the United Kingdom and the United States, social background is more substantially related to educational achievement than in the OECD as a whole.

The OECD classified participating countries according to quality, as indicated by results in reading, and equity, as indicated by the strength of the relationship between social background and achievement. Countries that are 'high quality' and 'high equity' are Canada, Finland, Hong Kong China, Iceland, Ireland, Japan, Korea and Sweden. In these countries there is no trade-off between quality and equity. Countries that are 'high quality' and 'low equity' include Australia, Belgium, France, New Zealand, the United Kingdom and the United States.

There has been a considerable amount of work that explains the findings about quality and equity. Reference was made in Chapter 3 to Finland and Alberta, the top performing province in Canada, with contributing factors including quality of teaching, strong support in the community for schools and level of funding. In these two instances there is a high degree of alignment among the different kinds of capital that are available to support schools. Many readers of this book reside in countries that are 'high quality' and 'low equity' and in this chapter and Chapter 7 we consider how the allocation of funds to schools can assist a shift to 'high quality' and 'high equity'.

The same kinds of analysis can be done at the system and school levels. In some schools, for example, the association between social background and student achievement is considerably weaker than it is for schools as a whole. The issue here is how these schools set their priorities and allocate all of their resources, including money. In Chapters 8 and 9 we describe a student-focused planning model that will make a contribution to a successful outcome for all schools.

Developments in Australia, especially Victoria, and the United Kingdom, especially England (and similar initiatives in New Zealand and some districts in Canada and the United States), demonstrate an acceptance that flexibility in planning and resource allocation is needed, given that there is a unique mix of learning needs in each school. This lies at the heart of practice in self-managing schools such that, as far as possible, funds are allocated directly to schools for local decision-making. To accomplish this, systems of education had to develop defensible methods to align school funding with the number and nature of students. It is now history that initial attempts were rudimentary at best, but the associated transparency of the allocations has underpinned a wave of reform addressing the appropriate funding of schools in the pursuit of improvement in learning outcomes.

Developments along these lines have continued in Victoria, which is a relatively large system of about 1,650 government (state) schools. The aim is to secure an alignment of the funds allocated to the school and the unique mix of local learning needs. As described above, the focus is on improving learning outcomes for all students and diminishing the disparity of outcomes between students, that is, to achieve 'high quality' and 'high equity'. 'High quality' is achieved in an educational system when all students maximise their potential to learn, and 'high equity' is achieved when the challenging environmental circumstances of any child do not detract from all children maximising their potential for learning, backed by the belief that all children have a capacity to succeed.

Seeking to align the funding of schools with these changing expectations means that alignment must be sought not only with the number and nature of students but also, importantly, with the learning needs of students, particularly with those needs that act as impediments to learning. Major attention in the development of funding models for self-managing schools has been given to the needs of children with impairments and disabilities. Funding has also taken account of socio-economic circumstances, language background, indigenous culture and isolation. However, children from these environments, particularly when these factors occur in combination, still predominate among those disengaging from schooling and/or failing to attain success prior to leaving. Not only is there a requirement to now address learning and teaching for these students, but there is also a requirement to determine appropriate funding mechanisms. This is now receiving attention in England and Victoria. The starting point for determining such a mechanism is a review of developments in secondary education. Victoria is selected for illustration.

State (government) provision in secondary education is a relatively recent phenomenon in Victoria, as in most parts of Australia. Following federation in 1901, education remained a state rather than federal responsibility and, although primary education was universal, secondary was certainly reserved for a few, who gained it in the main through non-government (private) schools. It was as recently as 2005 that the centenary of the first state government school was celebrated in Victoria (Melbourne High School). Expectations that all students would proceed to secondary schooling did not form until several decades later. Four phases can be discerned in these and subsequent developments.

Phase 1: Access. Beginning in the late 1930s, the expectation was that all students would gain access to secondary education. A programme of providing secondary schools in regional and rural areas began. However, it was accepted that these schools would vary greatly in the quality of educational provision. Major city schools competed with their longer-established private counterparts and were funded accordingly, but outer-suburban, regional and especially rural schools were indeed only second cousins or even further removed.

Phase 2: Opportunity. In the late 1950s expectations changed. It was acknowledged that all students should have equal opportunity to gain a quality education, irrespective of location and socio-economic circumstance. The emphasis was on 'opportunity' and this did not include provision to ensure that 'opportunity was grasped'. The opportunity expectation gave rise to the 'comprehensive secondary school'. At least minimum levels of educational provision were identified and established, resulting in a more even spread of resources.

Phase 3: Outcomes. Beginning in the late 1970s, the concept of equity of outcomes for students began to emerge, with the concept being defined as 'all students achieving or exceeding agreed standards'. It is emphasised that it 'began to emerge', as it has also taken many years for this new view of equity to become the expectation. It has been reflected in the diversification of schooling through flexibility and self-management to more effectively meet the needs of students, and certainly in endeavouring to allocate resources to schools by alignment, not only the number and nature of students as expressed through the stages of learning, but more importantly with the learning needs of students. This has certainly been a key endeavour in Victoria in recent years. This is emerging as the focus in resourcing schools – an unrelenting focus on student outcomes and allocating resources in congruence with student learning needs. There is an expectation that all students can achieve and that appropriate funding will assist. This focus is continuing as school systems seek to achieve the expectation of 'all across the line' or '90 per cent to successfully complete Year 12' or the like. However, achievement of the expectation is still some way off.

Phase 4: Aspirations. Thankfully, in education, we are never content with the present or even content with succeeding with current expectations before again pushing the boundaries on expectations. With many students still failing to achieve targets, the pursuit has begun to lift expectations to a new height, or even perhaps to a new dimension – enabling all students to achieve their aspirations. Of course, if this expectation is to be universal then it pre-supposes success with the previous expectation of all students achieving or exceeding targets in the basic outcomes. England is leading in this new era of expectation through the strategies of 'personalising learning' and 'school specialisation'. These strategies are important for all students, but particularly so for students at risk of disengaging from school prior to Year 12. It is with these students above all that choice and diversity need to be increased in relation to 'what is to be learnt' and 'how learning is to occur', to ensure curriculum and pedagogical relevance to the student. These strategies are becoming equally evident in Australia and are succinctly expressed through the priority of 'improving learning outcomes for all and decreasing (removing) disparity in outcome achievement'.

The relationship between needs and outcomes

The relationship between outcomes and needs is illustrated in Figure 6.1 which shows, on the vertical axis, the percentage of students achieving success, and on the horizontal axis, quintiles of increasing affluence in family socio-economic circumstance (diminishing student need). It is family circumstances, as expressed by the occupation of the main income earner, which is the best predictor of students most at risk of failing to benefit from educational opportunity.

The lower line typically illustrates the learning need–outcome relation for Year 12 students in educational jurisdictions in Australia and comparable countries. The upper line represents the required relationship if the commonly expressed target of '90 per cent of students to successfully complete Year 12' is to be achieved.

'Improving outcomes for all students and decreasing (removing) disparity' will require a major effort not only in curriculum, pedagogy and leadership but also in funding. It is readily apparent that the major endeavour will have to be in respect to the first three quintiles. It is also recognised that the effort and endeavour required increase exponentially as need increases. This relationship is illustrated in

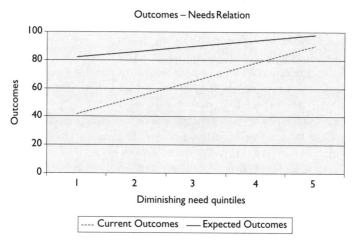

Figure 6.1 Relationship between current and expected outcomes (percentage achieving success) and need (quintiles) (figure devised by Jim Spinks).

Figure 6.2. The current and expected outcome lines have been retained in Figure 6.2 as illustrative only.

The challenge is to now fund students to pursue both equity of outcomes and achievement of aspirations through alignment of funding provision with expectations and the nature and needs of students. This higher level of educational expectations might be

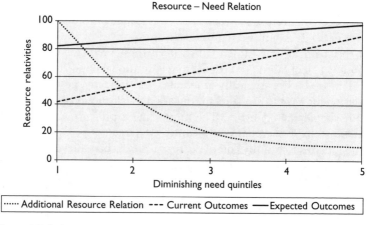

Figure 6.2 Relationship between resource relativities and need (figure devised by Jim Spinks).

termed 'aspirational' expectations. They are the key drivers for educational transformation.

The environment for educational change

We cannot ignore the fact that, while higher expectations may be the key driver of educational change, they work in unison with other factors within the overall education environment, including better practices in teaching and learning, the nature of schooling, and technology. This evolving educational environment is itself part of the similarly evolving social, political and economic environment. These environments are not separate but develop together in a 'symbiotic evolution', as illustrated in Figure 6.3.

It is within this relationship, driven by expectations for learning, that we must continually seek and correctly align the resourcing of student learning with the nature, number, interests, aptitudes and aspirations of students. Failure to do so will limit the achievement of expectations and perpetuate a climate in which failure for some students is accepted as inevitable.

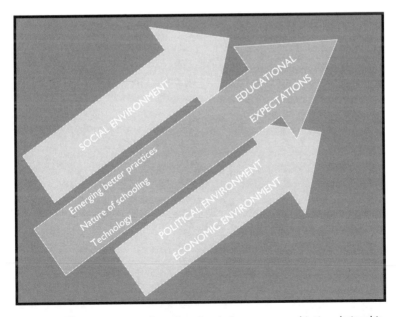

Figure 6.3 The environment for educational change – a symbiotic relationship (figure devised by Jim Spinks).

The way forward

This chapter shifted the focus to financial capital. The starting point was the contention that planning and resource allocation must be student focused if there is to be success for all students in all settings. Reference was made to the OECD's classification of countries based on results in PISA and the concern that just a small number offer education that is 'high quality' and 'high equity'. A brief historical account based on developments in Victoria, Australia illustrated how expectations are changing and that settling for less than 'high quality' and 'high equity' is no longer acceptable. Two sets of strategies must be developed: one is to determine a mechanism for allocating funds to schools in a manner that will maximise the opportunity to realise such an outcome. Such a mechanism must take account of factors that are predictors of student achievement. Promising approaches in Victoria are described in Chapter 6. The other is how funds once received are allocated at the school level. This strategy is addressed in subsequent chapters.

Chapter 7

Next practice in the funding of schools

Introduction

The concern in Chapter 7 is the alignment of funding with the nature and needs of students to achieve 'high quality' and 'high equity'. Particular attention is given to the approach in Victoria that drew from the findings of a research project proposed in *The Blueprint for Government Schools* (Department of Education and Training, 2003).

Framework for the allocation of funds to self-managing schools

A system of self-managing schools tends to allocate money to schools in the categories shown in Table 7.1. Most funds come from government, but included in Table 7.1 is provision for support from business, industry and philanthropic organisations, as well as parental contributions. The former (from business) is more prevalent in England while the latter (from parents) is a significant factor in Victoria. These developments are not without controversy, particularly in relation to fairness. The following observations can be made:

- The majority of resources are allocated by government, but the revenue streams from business, philanthropic organisations and parents are becoming increasingly important.
- Student-focused funding relates to the achievement of 'high quality' and 'high equity' on an ongoing basis. It is about the design, delivery and support of high value learning and teaching programmes.
- Core student learning relates to the number and nature of the students (stages of learning) to ensure the achievement of 'high

Table 7.1 Classification of budget categories for funding self-managing schools

			Core student learning	Can include: • the stages of learning and relativities between them • translation into per student funding • a base amount relating to diseconomies of scale	Can represent 75–90%
TOTAL SCHOOL FUNDING	Government Allocated Funding	Student Focused Funding	Equity	Can include: • disabilities and impairments • socio-economic status • language background • isolated location • mobility • indigenous	5–10%
		School Based Funding	Targeted initiatives	• targeted to specific schools or programmes, usually for specified periods of time • often awarded through 'bids' or submissions • can be closely related to political agendas	2–10%
			Infrastructure operation and maintenance	Can include: • utilities • maintenance • minor development	3–5%

		Infrastructure ownership	• buildings and grounds major development	0 + %
Non-Gov Funding		Specific initiatives or provisions	• often targeted to specific initiatives • can be supplied 'as cash or in kind' • an increasingly important source of funding • parent contributions	0 + %

quality'. It should enable all students from supportive environments to achieve their learning potential.

• Equity relates to the extraordinary needs of the students, that is, those factors that can impede students from achieving their learning potential. The allocation of funds intended to improve equity is usually linked to overcoming the identified impediments and is derived from the degree and density of occurrence of the impeding factor. Allocation is usually formula-driven, as practice demonstrates that allocation through bids or submissions is no guarantee that the resource will end up in the schools with the students of greatest need. In fact the opposite has been observed.

Designing a student-focused funding model

This section proposes a strategy for systems to review the allocation of resources to schools to enable the achievement of student potential. It recognises that students with extraordinary needs related to disabilities and impairments and/or their environment and background require further funding, which will be considered in the section on resourcing equity.

The strategies will be of particular interest in England, where the allocation of resources to schools is still based on Age Weighted Pupil Units (AWPU) and Free School Meals (FSM) as an indicator of socio-economic disadvantage, with bidding for additional resources to address other needs and take up particular opportunities. These approaches do not hold up under critical scrutiny. The strategies that follow may be worthy of consideration in the identification of 'next practice' in the resourcing of schools.

A key feature of the proposed strategies is that the evidence that underpins them is gathered from schools that are not only highly effective and efficient in significantly and systematically adding value to student learning outcomes, but which also exhibit the characteristics of sustainability in the future. Participating schools should exhibit the characteristics of best practice in teaching and learning and a culture of continually and avidly doing even better. It is proposed that patterns of resource deployment in these schools provide the exemplars for the design of models for use across a system.

It is acknowledged at the outset that past practices in resource allocation were mostly historically based, with many embedded features that were unfair and unsustainable. Even with the development of systems of self-managing schools and related approaches to school global budgets, history had been a major factor in deriving allocation formulae. For instance, mythology had insisted that the age of the student should be a major driver of resourcing and that resource provision needed to increase with age. Although to some degree this myth has been shattered in relation to the early years of learning, it persists in the middle years and governs differentiation within the senior years. Perusal of the AWPUs of most local education authorities in England supports this conclusion, with relativities in early years typically around 1.3 decreasing to 1.0 in late primary, but increasing from 1.3 to 1.6 or more in senior secondary. The question needs to be asked whether this pattern reflects best practice in the expenditure of resources in schools achieving high quality.

Of course some would ask 'Does it matter?' if the school is free to deploy resources as it sees fit, in the best interests of students. The answer is 'Yes', especially if there is a significant funding differential across the stages of learning or age-grades and the proportional mix of students across these categories differs from school to school. This was evident in Victoria where, historically, Years 11 and 12 students were funded at a higher level but schools spread this resource across all secondary year groups. This meant that schools with higher proportions of students in Years 11 and 12 were advantaged and yet it was the schools with the lower proportions of students in Years 11 and 12 that desperately needed more resources to address the root causes of students disengaging and not continuing to the final years. It was evident that disengagement did not just occur at the end of Year 10 but over Years 9 and 10. A similar situation was evident in South Australia, where funding also favoured the more senior years and yet research demonstrated that school expenditure was relatively flat across secondary classes and, in some large high schools with high proportions of students in Years 11–12, expenditure on Year 12 was the lowest on a per student basis.

These examples illustrate the desirability of reviewing and redesigning funding models on the basis of evidence of what occurs in schools that plan well in matching their resources to priorities for learning. In the past it has been difficult to obtain evidence on the relative costs of education across year groups. This problem has been solved by analysis of expenditure patterns in representative samples of leading-edge schools known to add value to student learning. Central to this analysis has been consideration of how learning and teaching are delivered and supported, rather than a simple financial analysis. In essence, information is obtained about learning and teaching which can then be translated into time units and costs. The outcome is the cost per student in relation to year groups (or other groups of choice) that accurately expresses how the school has chosen to deploy the resources available to it.

Guidelines

The following guidelines propose a strategy for aligning the allocation of core student learning resources in a student-focused funding model with the number and nature of students, using evidence gained from leading-edge schools which are systematically adding significant value to student learning.

- The design of a model for the allocation of funds to schools in self-managing systems should be based on evidence from schools, as it is at the school level that constantly changing educational and socio-political environments, expressed through ever-increasing expectations, have implications for student funding.
- School principals are the critical participants in gathering evidence, as they are in the best position to know the implications of changing expectations for student funding (the pre-eminent leadership position in education is that of principal).

- Evidence of resource deployment should be sought through a focus on how people/programmes contribute to learning and teaching or the support of learning and teaching, and not through simple financial analysis.
- Information should be gathered from schools that are representative of type, size, location and socio-economic circumstance, and that are known to significantly, systematically and sustainably add value to student learning outcomes.
- These schools should exhibit best practice in learning and teaching and in those characteristics related to the nature of schooling as it is likely to evolve in the future.
- These schools should exhibit a culture of continually and avidly seeking better practice.
- Evidence should include analysis of all activities that enhance or support learning, irrespective of the source of the related funding.
- There may be a need to consider compensation for diseconomies of scale for some schools through the application of variable base allocations.
- Parallel evidence should be sought from a random sample of schools to ascertain whether there is a relationship between school nature, student performance and school resource deployment patterns.
- Resource provision should be driven by the recipients of schooling and this should be reflected in allocation models.
- Models should ensure maximum flexibility for schools to deploy resources as expectations and the educational environment change.
- Any resource allocation model can only reflect the expectations and environment of the 'near' future. There is a need to update evidence and refine models on at least a triennial basis.

Resourcing quality

The resourcing of schools to ensure that all students achieve success at the level of their potential calls for alignment of resources and the number and nature of students in the context of emerging best practice in learning and teaching. The following is a summary of developments in efforts to resource quality:

- Educational funding is shifting from funding schools to funding students, and relating that funding to the nature, needs, aptitudes and aspirations of students.

- Student funding should directly relate to changing expectations for learning, emerging better practices in learning and teaching and the evolving nature of schooling.
- The focus of data collection in the first instance must be clearly on the nature and quality of the delivery and support of learning and teaching, rather than on the cost implications of these activities.
- Changing expectations for student learning are part of an evolving complex of inter-related social, political, economic and technological developments. Strategies should continuously generate responsive models for educational resource allocation.
- Resource allocation models should look forwards and not backwards or sideways. The best source of data is to be found in leading-edge schools where the characteristics of the future are already being exhibited in outcomes, practices and intentions.
- Principals as educational leaders are the best source of information, as they grapple daily with the relationships between expectations, best available practices, outcomes, available resources and future requirements.
- Comprehensive data bases within school systems are enabling resource allocation models to be developed on evidence rather than hypothesis and history.

Resourcing equity

'High equity' is achieved when all students achieve good educational outcomes irrespective of their background and circumstance. Typically, it is students from low socio-economic family circumstances, English as a second language (ESL) backgrounds and those living in isolated rural areas who are overly represented among those disengaging from school prior to Year 12, or who are not achieving good educational outcomes at the completion of Year 12. For these students the commencement of school is often hampered by limited language skills, low aspirations and expectations and a restricted range of experiences on which to construct learning. These problems can be exacerbated for older students by frequent school changes, a lack of or poor prior school experiences and a social environment where learning is under-valued. Their life chances are not positive and achieving good educational outcomes is fundamental to reversing this situation.

Achieving high equity and removing the disparity in educational outcomes between students on the basis of environment has become the moral and social imperative of our time. It requires outstanding alignment of resources with learning needs. To date substantial funds have been spent, but whether these are sufficient or correctly targeted is unknown in many settings. What is known is that these students are still overly represented amongst our failing students.

Ruth Kelly, former Secretary of State for Education and Skills, set the challenge, as quoted in Chapter 6 – 'a rock solid belief that all children can achieve' and a 'conviction that every child . . . deserves a good education'. Consistent with Kelly's call for moral purpose and social justice, David Hopkins in his keynote presentation at the 13th National Conference of the Specialist Schools and Academies Trust in November 2005 further challenged the system to boldly devise a strategy to 'equalise life chances by tilting against inequality, with innovation and collaboration to improve standards' and to provide 'sufficient funding, devolved to school level and allocated to need' (Hopkins, 2005). In his opening address at the same conference, Sir Cyril Taylor, Chair of the Specialist Schools and Academies Trust, issued the same challenge to provide for the most vulnerable children.

A commitment to ensure that all students successfully complete their secondary education is not yet at the top of priorities in the agenda for educational reform. To date, the focus has been on maximising the learning potential of every student. This has produced remarkable progress, particularly in England, in encouraging schools to ensure that larger numbers of students achieve at least five good grades at GCSE. This endeavour has tended to focus the attention of schools on those students perceived as being at risk of performing at just below the 'five good grades' criterion. It is time to include students at risk in the lowest orders of achievement and ensure that their achievement is improved above and beyond an acceptable minimum standard of learning outcomes.

The student resource package in Victoria

Victoria is an example of a system that wishes to achieve a stronger alignment of student-focused funding and success for all students. It requires some fundamental re-thinking about engagement, curriculum, pedagogy and resourcing.

Research project

In April 2003, the Expenditure Review Committee (ERC) of the Victorian Department of Premier and Cabinet initiated the development of a student-focused school funding model, based on stages of schooling and equity component benchmarks. The project became known as the Student Resource Package Research Project. A key purpose of the project was to determine the elements, relativities and educational rationale underpinning the provision of equity funding, with the longer-term goal of ensuring that 90 per cent of all students successfully complete Year 12.

The University of Melbourne was commissioned to undertake a project to establish the necessary benchmarks and develop a new student-focused resource allocation model to be implemented for 2005. The research project was led by Professor Richard Teese from the Faculty of Education, assisted by Associate Professor Stephen Lamb and Senior Fellow Jim Spinks.

Methodology

Effective schools were identified by aggregating a number of performance indicators for groups of schools with similar student intake characteristics (socio-economic and location). Performance indicators were averaged over a period of two to three years, depending on data availability. Indicators for secondary schools included student retention, student absence, Victorian Certificate of Education (VCE) scores, post-Year 12 transition and teacher morale. For primary schools the indicators were AIM (Assessment Improvement Monitor) scores in key learning areas for Years 3 and 5. For each indicator, the residual value between the expected and observed outcome was determined, taking into account the influence of student intake and contextual factors. An aggregate measure of effectiveness was created by summing the residuals for each school. Efficient schools were those operating on a 'least cost' per student basis. Items over which schools did not have management control and/or were included in school budgets as an administrative convenience were excluded. A representative sample of 42 effective and efficient schools was selected by merging data on effective schools with data on efficient schools, grouped according to size of school. Atypical schools were excluded.

Data were gathered on site to establish per student expenditure patterns across the year groups within the school. All inputs were converted to per student costs. These inputs included teaching, organisation, management, leadership, care and wellbeing, counselling, planning, materials and equipment. The process called for the mapping of each individual's contribution, as agreed in discussions with the principal; conversion of the activity contribution map to a time analysis in relation to student year groups; and determination of a per student cost by translating time against a salary or programme cost. Summation of total contributions established the patterns of resource deployment in relation to selected groupings of students.

A more detailed account of how the information gathered in this process was used in determining allocations to schools is available from the Department of Education and Training (DET, n.d.). A summary of the funding mechanism, updated to 2007, is contained in Appendix 5 (Department of Education and Training, Victoria, 2006).

Critical issues

A critical aspect in developing the student-focused resource allocation model was the funding of students with different learning needs. This aspect of the project was addressed by Stephen Lamb, whose research (Lamb, 2004) identified the factors that are significant predictors of failure. (Lamb and Teese (2003) did not recoil from the use of the word 'failure'; it is the eradication of failure that was the overarching intention). These factors were low socio-economic status, disabilities and impairments, rural location, English as a second language, mobility, indigenous students and small school size.

Lamb (2004) offered the following points to guide the development of a student-focused funding model:

- Any need factor is not randomly distributed across schools but concentrated in particular communities and schools.
- The density of incidence of a need factor within a school population is critical to the overall impact on student performance.
- A multiplicity of high density impediments often occurs, particularly in schools serving low socio-economic communities.
- Effort required to overcome these impediments increases exponentially as density of occurrence increases within the school.
- Although impediments inter-relate, separate targeting is required.
- Resourcing does make a difference.

- In general, past equity allocations were insufficient and spread too thinly across schools to be effective.

Implications for other countries

The Victorian approach to equity in resource allocation contrasts with developments in other places such as England, where there is a greater emphasis on schools 'bidding' for additional resources. If this bidding is restricted to those schools considered eligible on the basis of student characteristics, then it is appropriate to obtain prior agreement on intended deployment and accountability require-ments. However, there is an inherent problem of some schools with high needs students being differentially funded. If student-focused funding is to be pursued as a means of supporting student-focused outcomes and student-focused learning, then it follows that student-focused funding should be strongly related to the nature and needs of the students, irrespective of their location, rather than on the cap-acity of the school to win at bidding. There is also the question of resource guarantee to underpin confidence in long-term planning, as dramatically and sustainably changing the outcomes for high needs students is a long-term process.

Bidding for resources to explore better learning and teaching practices through innovation is more appropriate. In this instance it is usually recognised that good practice is already in place, but there is a strong desire to identify even better practice.

The pursuit of equity or diminishing the disparity of outcomes between students is dependent on additional resources. As David Hopkins (2005) stated, it requires 'a strategy to equalise life chances by tilting against inequality, with innovation and collaboration to improve standards' and 'sufficient funding, devolved to school level and allocated to need'. The following guidelines are offered for the development of student-focus funding models that take account of evidence on the achievement of equity.

- The development of up-to-date and comprehensive data bases of school characteristics and performance is essential for investigating and improving resource allocation models to ensure the maximisation of the learning potential of every student.
- These data bases enable hypotheses about learning outcomes and funding models to be tested and established on the basis of

evidence. There should be evidence to support any resource allocation model currently in use.

- Resource models to allocate student-focused funding should enable specific targeting in congruence with the needs of the individual student.

- Optimum model development requires the identification of specific indices for each category of need that accurately predict those students most at risk, enable differentiation between degrees of need and provide congruent funding allocations. Complex, multi-faceted indices can obscure the importance of a specific need for an individual student or school.

- Indices of need to drive resource allocation formulae should be continuous functions, to avoid threshold points where significant changes in resources can occur as a result of minor changes in the value of the index.

- Base data for an index of need should be averaged over a suitable number of years to reduce the impact of atypical fluctuations.

- Base data for an index of need should relate to the students attending the school and not the geographic location of the school.

- There is recognition that degree of need, density of incidence of students with that need within the school, and endurance of the need within the school over time are all factors to be considered in allocating funds.

- Student-focused funding should be allocated on the basis of formulae driven processes to ensure transparency, fairness and equity and be dependent on the needs of students rather than the capacity of the school to bid for resources.

- Student-focused funding models need to be continually updated through review of impact on the learning outcomes of students.

Resourcing for special or additional needs

The initial research in Victoria to develop a new student-focused model for allocating resources to schools did not address the needs of students with additional or special needs. This was a separate and subsequent project. The special needs of these students differ from the categories of need considered previously, in that they are the outcome of the 'chances of birth' and are mostly unrelated to socio-economic and other family circumstances. These needs include physical and intellectual disabilities and sensory behaviour, learning and autistic spectrum disorders, as well as mental illnesses. Typically, each of these occur across a range of expressions from normal to mild to moderate to severe to profound.

For the past decade 'students with disabilities and impairments' have been funded on a per student basis using a model which identifies firstly, the stage of schooling of the student and secondly, the level of disability. The three stages of schooling, relation to age and the 2006 allocation are given in Table 7.2.

Table 7.2 Stage of schooling disability allocation in Victoria (2006)

Stage	Age	Allocation per student (AU$)
1	5–10	$5,397
2	11–16	$3,859
3	17–18	$4,247

The major component is the level of disability allocation, determined on the basis of responses to an Educational Needs Questionnaire (ENQ). This allocation is divided into six levels in relation to increasing levels of need, as indicated in Table 7.3.

Table 7.3 Educational Needs Questionnaire (ENQ) allocations in Victoria (2006)

ENQ level	Allocation per student (AU$)
1	$4,886
2	$11,300
3	$17,838
4	$24,346
5	$30,803
6	$37,292

Minor differences in allocations occur, depending on whether the student is enrolled in a special or mainstream school. Allocations along the lines illustrated in Table 7.2 are similar to the pioneering approach in Edmonton, Canada, commencing in the late 1970s.

Although the Victorian model has served its purpose as a student-focused approach, dissatisfaction has been growing within the profession in relation to the accuracy of the ENQ in assessing the support required to achieve the desired outcomes for these high needs students. There is also dissatisfaction emanating from the negative focus of the ENQ on 'what the child cannot do' as well as consistency of assessments.

The disquiet with the ENQ and the provision for students with additional or special needs in Victoria is addressed in the work of a Ministerial Advisory Group. Its functions include the initiation of research into the funding of special needs, the review of all pro-grammes for students with special needs and the identification of measures to better align per student resourcing with the nature and needs of students.

The disquiet in relation to provisions for students with special needs in Victoria is paralleled in the United Kingdom. Several reviews have been undertaken, with reports including *Removing Barriers to Achievement: The Government's Strategy for Special Education Needs* (DfES, 2004b), *Special Education Needs Report* (House of Commons Education and Skills Committee, 2006) and *Special Educational Needs and Disability: Towards Inclusive Schools* (Ofsted, 2004).

The current concern in Victoria and England centres not only on funding but also on the very nature of 'inclusive' education for students with special needs. Too often this term is narrowly considered to mean all students with special needs attending mainstream schools. Recent reviews are clarifying the matter, with the definition of 'inclusive education' becoming more comprehensive. The following definition is representative of emerging views:

> Inclusive education provides opportunities for children with additional needs to enrol in a variety of school settings. It is characterised by a blurring of the boundaries between children with and those without additional learning needs, so that the focus is on:
>
> • the level of capacity to learn and progress that each individual possesses

- the learning outcomes sought
- the environment and support which the school that the child attends (regardless of type) undertakes to provide.

The delivery of genuinely inclusive practices will be system-wide. Schools will welcome diversity among their students and demonstrate exceptional skills in personalising their learning pathways, to maximise learning and wellbeing outcomes for all.

Such definitions highlight the growing preference in the field of special education to move from a deficit or negative approach to funding special student needs to a model based on the capacities that the students bring with them. It is recognised that current approaches to funding developed from emotional overbalancing following decades of political and social neglect. It has resulted in funding models whereby the allocation increases in direct proportion to the number of deficits identified. Principals often describe the trauma for parents and teachers in assessment sessions, where the emphasis is on the identification of as many deficits for learning as possible to maximise funding. This approach certainly does not assist the initial development of positive feelings and confidence. It also does not assist in finding the way forward for the student in terms of learning.

There is a growing preference for developing models based on the capacities that these students individually bring to the learning process as the starting point for efforts to optimise their learning and wellbeing in general. This preference suggests the possibility of an approach along the following lines:

- Initial acceptance of a student with a disability into special needs programmes based on medical or clinical evidence and diagnosis.
- Assessment of the student's capacities/capabilities for learning and the establishment of related learning and wellbeing targets.
- Proposal of a potential pathway to these outcomes, taking into account developmental risk factors, and with associated funding determined by reference to a set of standard pathways identified through research of existing successful pathways.
- Capacities/capabilities, outcome targets, potential pathways and

developmental risk factors would be assessed by professional agencies from outside the special education provider group.

- Independent reviews would be conducted on a triennial basis.

Although this preference is attractive, particularly as there is an emphasis on learning and wellbeing outcomes, with the existing capacities of the student as the starting point, it is acknowledged that the initial assessment process would be expensive. As well, the identification of a set of standard pathways and the associated support requirements would need extensive research to glean data from successful wellbeing and learning outcome programmes.

It is possible that the assessment cost could be substantially diminished by limiting assessment to those students medically or clinically identified as being in the moderate/severe to profound range of the disability or disorder. There is evidence that the occurrence of students within the mild/moderate range can more readily be predicted on census-based population distributions, with modification for known distribution patterns within populations. This allows the allocation of available resources directly to schools, with further modification in relation to stages of schooling to enhance early intervention capacities.

The outcome could be the development of a funding model where the allocation for the student with special needs is sufficient to ensure the optimal achievement of learning and wellbeing outcomes identified as being the potential of the student, based on their capacities for learning and personal development and growth. This allocation would be irrespective of the type or category of disability or disorder. The focus would be on the potential of the student for learning, growth and development.

The exploration of capacity-based models for students with special needs to replace current deficit based models is in its infancy. There are attractive features, but further work is required to determine validity and gain the necessary support of parents and special education providers.

The way forward

The next step for Victoria is to align resources and aspirations. There is a view that student aspiration encompasses what is to be learnt and how learning is to occur. It is closely allied with the concepts of personalising learning and school specialisation, where it is envisaged that new curriculum as well as changed pedagogy could be the outcome. This differs in some ways from personalising learning and specialisation in England, where the emphasis is more strongly on establishing personal learning targets and changing pedagogy, but within the confines of existing curriculum structure. Both approaches have strengths and there is a case for each to be considered by the other, particularly in relation to the capacity within Victoria to establish personal learning targets regarding processes and outcomes.

Chapter 8

A student-focused planning model

Introduction

Ensuring that all students secure success and attain the necessary skills and capacities to lead successful and productive lives requires an alignment of funding and these intended outcomes. This imperative lay at the heart of Chapter 7, where the issue was the manner in which resources are allocated to schools in a self-managing system. However, ensuring that schools are sufficiently and appropriately funded is only the beginning. It is then the responsibility of the principal and others in the school community to ensure that the resources that have been allocated are deployed in the most effective and efficient ways possible to enable expectations for each and every student to be realised.

It is important to reiterate that money alone does not guarantee outcomes on the scale of transformation. It is but one element in the matrix of high quality teaching, relevant and challenging curriculum, appropriate pedagogy, community support and trust, along with masterful leadership and good governance that includes effective and efficient management of resources. This is the unifying theme of the book and central to the model for alignment set out in Chapter 3.

The purpose of this chapter is to describe a model to guide the deployment of resources at the school level in a manner that ensures that the student is at the centre of the process. We describe this as a student-focused planning model. The need for such a model is consistent with the new enterprise logic of schools set out in Chapter 1. Two important elements are that 'the student is the most important unit of organisation' and 'new approaches to the allocation of resources are required'.

The journey so far

Our earlier work on self-managing schools yielded models for policy-making, planning and budgeting that seemed well suited to the times (Caldwell and Spinks, 1988; 1992; 1998). However, Brian Caldwell's work in the early 2000s, as self-managing schools become part of the scene in places like Australia, England and New Zealand, led to the view that it is time for the concept of self-management to catch up with its best practice. Schools are doing remarkable things with their new authorities and responsibilities. He drew implications for leadership in *Re-imagining Educational Leadership* (Caldwell, 2006).

At the same time, Jim Spinks was engaged in research and development in Victoria and South Australia that led to a new framework for allocating resources to schools within self-managing systems, along the lines set out in Chapter 7. He gathered evidence of how principals and other leaders at the school level were deploying those resources in imaginative ways that focused more than ever on the needs, interests, aptitudes and aspirations of students. He also noted progress in England. We pooled our knowledge to see how schools in these different settings were drawing on four sources of capital as they went about their work, and this led to the model of alignment that frames the book. We now complete the picture by explaining and illustrating a student-focused planning model. In essence, we are 're-imagining the resourcing of schools'.

Design parameters

The student-focused planning model was designed with the following parameters in mind:

1   The student and his/her learning should be the focus. The student should be the starting point for planning and the basis on which to allocate resources and evaluate the outcomes.
2   Models should reflect emerging best practice in exemplary value-adding schools.
3   Models are not just a recipe, they provide frameworks for identifying the many activities that ought to take place within a school.
4   It is important that the relationship between the many activities is clearly identified.

5   Models should reflect how a school works over a period of years, as well as on a day-to-day basis.

6   Models should reflect the pattern of leadership across the school and how people work together in teams.

7   Models should be straightforward and easily understood, as a key purpose for them is to explain how a school makes decisions.

8   Models are frameworks, not detailed management strategies to be imposed on schools. Their main function is to encourage and assist schools to develop their own approaches that identify and explain how the school operates.

In essence, a model for school planning identifies key activities and the relationships among them. These activities range from setting individual learning targets for students, to monitoring the achievement of those targets and student wellbeing, to creating strategic alliances in support of the effort, to designing and delivering curriculum, to creating school budgets, to celebrating success and everything in between.

These parameters and a range of major activities have been brought together in the model in Figure 8.1. It is not intended to be the definitive model, but a starting point to assist schools in the design of their own approach.

The student, as an individual, is the focus of the model, both at the beginning of the planning process and at the point at which intended learning outcomes are identified and used as the basis for learning and teaching as well as programme evaluation. The student and his/her characteristics are also considered in the context of *values, purposes and expectations*, as these might be endorsed by a leadership team or governing body. Alignment is intended but, if there are divergences, then at least they need to be known, understood and accepted by all parties.

The student is viewed as central to *school strategic planning* but, more importantly, to a process of *student personalised planning* to ensure relevance of curriculum and pedagogy to the characteristics and expectations for the student's learning. School strategic planning remains a necessary activity to effectively plan future changes and address long-term issues. This planning needs to reflect trends in expectations for learning and performance in relation to those expectations.

Student personalised planning and school strategic planning provide the basis for *designing curriculum* and *planning for student access* to a curriculum of relevance to learning targets. This may well involve

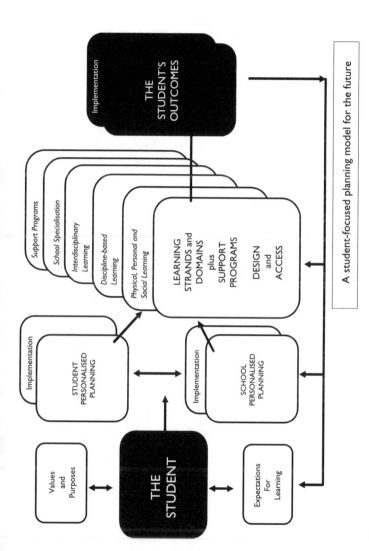

Figure 8.1 Student-focused planning model.

the construction of new curriculum in the school to meet the specific requirements for learning for a particular student. This is a test of the priority the school places on personalising learning. The model illustrated in Figure 8.1 refers to three *learning strands* with the possibility of further division into sub-categories or *domains*. The terminology reflects that of the Victorian Essential Learning Standards (VELS), the new curriculum for students in primary and lower secondary in Victoria (Victorian Curriculum and Assessment Authority, 2005). For England, these would be replaced with the ten Key Learning Areas (KLAs) from the national curriculum. The model also includes a program of specialisation and a group of support programmes which could include ICT, library, administration, buildings and grounds. Planning for each programme would include targets, content, delivery, resources and approaches to evaluation.

The student's outcomes provide the basis for monitoring progress and assessing the performance of the individual student and, collectively, the basis for the review and evaluation of learning and teaching programmes and programmes that support them.

It should be noted that student personalised planning, school strategic planning and the student's outcomes are backed by 'implementation' indicators. Similarly, 'implementation' becomes a key aspect for the programmes identified in learning and teaching and that support learning and teaching. The requirement for resources to implement each programme includes consideration of student learning time, learning space and the financial implications for human resources and material support. Planning should emphasise the relationship of resource requirements to learning targets and priorities. The sum of the programme implementation plans would form the proposed school budget. If the sum exceeds availability, then a review of targets and priorities informs the balancing process.

This overview of the model is intentionally brief to help develop understanding of the model as student focused and different from past models, with their focus on the school as a collection of classrooms rather than individual students. Each component and its relationship to the model in general are now described in more detail.

Details of the model

The student-focused planning model described in this section considers the student to be the most important unit in the organisation. The mission of the school is to ensure that all students secure success and that disparities between students' achievements are diminished. All activities are focused on this endeavour. Planning starts with the student's expectations for learning and finishes with the student's outcomes. In between, there is an intensity of curriculum design and delivery, with constant monitoring and guidance of the student's progress.

The model is not intended to be the definitive model, but an example. Schools are encouraged to develop their own models that reflect the unique and distinct characteristics of their own circumstances.

The student

The model begins with 'the student'. This refers to each and every student and his/her family, undertaking a process of school choice and possible entry.

The nature, needs, interests, aptitudes, current attainments and future aspirations of the student are central to the process, both in terms of the student and his/her family and the school. Even within the scope of unlimited imagination, a school cannot be all things to all people. For this reason it is also important to include the major activities and related statements of 'Values and Purposes' and 'Expectations for Learning', as these traditionally have been used by schools and their governing bodies to describe key characteristics and by parents to ascertain the suitability of the school in relation to the beliefs, values and aspirations of the family. In the past, the emphasis has been on what the school can offer the student, subject to the view that all students will in the main follow a similar path. In the future, the focus becomes: 'Given the nature, needs, interests, aptitudes, current attainments and aspirations of the student, what outcomes can the school envisage as a set of realistic expectations for the student while attending the school?' This approach is now evident at schools like Lymm High School in Cheshire and de Ferrers Specialist Technology College in Burton on Trent.

The student and his/her individual characteristics and expectations are the starting point for school planning. This contrasts with the declining practice of providing all students with a common curriculum and expectations, with some modification as the student progresses through the school. This leap to addressing personal expectations for learning, based on individual targets that are realistic and achievable, is a vital outcome of current reform in England. It is recommended that other countries examine these developments if they wish to pursue the personalising of learning. Without personal targets as the starting point, personalised learning is restricted to what is learnt and how it is learnt rather than being inclusive of why, to what purpose and for which expected outcomes.

Personalising student learning from the very beginning of entry to a school, based on the current attainments of the student as well as the nature, needs, interests, aptitudes and aspirations of the student, is fundamental to pre-school to Year 12 being a smooth continuum of learning and development. Too often the transition from one school to another (and even from one year group to another) has become a disruption to the student and detrimental to his/her overall school achievement.

Values and purposes

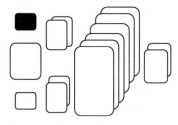

Schools cannot be all things to all people. Even with the student as the most important unit in the organisation, there is still the need for the school to clearly articulate a set of values and purposes about children and their learning and development. This statement is usually a key part of the school charter or mission and often developed jointly by the school principal, staff and community through the governing body. There needs to be agreement and commitment to these values and purposes. They also become a key reference point for the resolution of difficulties in the planning of change.

Expectations for learning

Well articulated statements of expectations for learning have become important in planning for schools. They help shape national standards for student learning, as well as local priorities. The development of a capacity in schools in England to quantify what value is to be added in relation to student learning and to set school-wide targets for value adding is a significant advance. Too often 'value-adding' has remained a concept that could be claimed but not demonstrated.

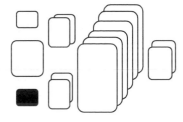

In late 2005, Jim Spinks visited Lymm High School in Cheshire and Bishop Walsh Catholic School and Turves Green Boys' Technical School in Birmingham. All three schools demonstrated significant 'value added' through the percentage of students achieving or exceeding five good GCSE passes or their equivalent in relation to expectation. Even more impressive was the fact that this significant value-adding was sustained over several years and had become an important aspect of school ethos. Students 'expected to exceed expectations'!

It is proposed that an 'inclusive ethos' be an expectation for learning. An 'inclusive ethos' expresses the expectation that all students will be included in learning outcome success. It is based on the belief that 'all children have the capacity to learn' and that all students can achieve or exceed a benchmark standard that will enable them to successfully participate in society. This expectation underpins the Victorian and South Australian targets that 90 per cent of students will successfully complete Years 12 or 13 or their equivalent. It is also strongly expressed by former Secretary of State Ruth Kelly (2005) as 'a rock solid belief that all children can achieve' and by Minister Jacqui Smith (2005) as a target 'to increase the number of 16 year olds participating in learning from 75 per cent to 90 per cent'.

As illustrated by the three schools above, many English schools are excelling in adding value as measured by the percentages of students exceeding the expectation for those gaining at least five good GCSE passes, with the expectation based on student attainments at entry. The amendment in 2006 of the 'five good GCSE passes' benchmark to include English and mathematics is welcomed. The challenge is also to establish a minimum set of standards, the attainment of which will indicate the likelihood of successful participation of each and every student in society.

Student personalised learning

With student individual characteristics and expectations the starting point for school planning, strategic planning remains a key activity for the principal and staff for planning in the medium to long term. However, even more important is the activity of 'Student Personalised Planning' to determine the expectations to be agreed for each student.

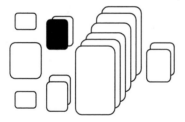

Based on the student's current attainments, realistic targets can be set using the available data bases that can assist in correlating current attainment and future expectations. The development of these data bases is an impressive aspect of current education reform in England.

The endeavours in other countries to personalise learning are severely limited by the lack of a capacity to set individual learning targets that relate to the nature, needs, interests, aptitudes, current attainments and aspirations of the student and that are evidence based. The development of a central data base of student characteristics and achievements to enable realistic targets to be set for each student, based on the achievements of other students with similar profiles, adds a dimension of reality to the task of individual target setting. These targets not only enable measures of value added to be made but, even more importantly, provide an incentive for student learning that is personal rather than merely aiming at a national benchmark.

It is evident that the development of a student characteristic and outcome achievement central data base, with some 600,000 new students added on an annual basis, is a fundamental underpinning of education reform in England. Other countries intent on similar reform would be well advised to consider the development of a similar data base a high priority.

Learning targets should also reflect the needs of the student and his/her aspirations for learning and through learning. The educational targets set for the student should also take account of the student's capacity for personal growth and development.

In the broader sense, student personalised planning is not only an activity to set appropriate learning targets for each student, but also to plan for support and monitoring of the student's progress towards those targets. This involves planning for counselling, exercising choice, coaching, mentoring and celebrating success. Student personalised planning also involves planning for access to relevant curriculum and ensuring that the desired learning occurs. This contrasts with the past, where this kind of attention was given to students after the onset of failure, not as a strategy to ensure that failure does not occur. For every school, this enhanced responsibility is a tall order. It cannot be effectively undertaken after problems arise, as the student may well have already wasted precious learning time moving down the wrong pathways. It needs to become central to school operation, perhaps initially with those students identified as being most at risk, as the school develops the capacity for undertaking this activity.

Many schools have attempted to include these approaches to personal planning in student home groups, with a teacher taking on this responsibility for 25–30 students. Some have been successful, but insufficient in respect to the time that is required if each and every student is to optimise his/her learning potential and all students are to successfully complete Years 12 or13.

Student personalised planning is not an activity that can be treated as an 'add-on'. It needs to become a key pathway to curriculum design and delivery and learning support. For this reason the model proposes that an implementation plan should be developed on an annual basis to underpin the activity, with this plan identifying purposes, guidelines, activities, resources and evaluation strategies.

It is similarly proposed that leadership of student personalised planning should become the responsibility of a senior member of staff, working with a team that includes some of the best teachers. An impressive approach along these lines has been implemented at Lymm High School in Cheshire.

Lymm High School, with approximately 2,000 students, is proud of its reputation for high quality and annually having 90 per cent of its students achieve five good passes at GCSE. Headteacher Roger Lounds explained to Jim Spinks that this was the outcome of the school's 'warp and weft' approach to student care. A meeting with the three heads of Key Stages quickly demonstrated the intensity and zeal with which the school pursued the achievement of student personal targets for learning, with comprehensive ongoing monitoring and mentoring programmes. Another meeting with the five heads of halls (each hall included students from Years 7 to 13) also demonstrated the high degree of care and support extended to students. High quality programmes of monitoring, counselling, mentoring and celebrating were in evidence. The weave of the many layers of safety nets was very tight indeed.

Schools often endeavour to provide this level and quality of support through one line of activity and responsibility. The 'warp and weft' approach at Lymm may well be more expensive in terms of leadership and teacher time, but the outcomes speak for themselves. It was also interesting to investigate whether there could be tension between the zeal for target-setting and compassion for children. An assistant head teacher explained that the two aspects of support quickly joined for a student in crisis. This meant that student well-being was pre-eminent, but every endeavour was also made to support the student in maintaining learning progress, as time lost from learning is nigh impossible to retrieve. Roger Lounds and the Lymm team have certainly re-imagined their own student-focused school. The fact that it is a large school, yet has developed a truly supportive school environment, is to their credit.

Outwood Grange College in Wakefield, with 1,800 students, is another outstanding school, with a special emphasis on personalising student planning to ensure that all students optimise their potential for learning and developing. Strategic leadership positions – Director of Performance and Director of Quality Assurance – are designed around support for students. It is interesting to compare these positions with the more traditional senior appointments related to curriculum areas.

Michael Wilkins, the Headteacher of Outwood Grange, is passionate and eloquent in explaining the details of its 'Praising Stars' programme, which centres on information gathering, identifying where a difference can be made, intervening systematically and making an impact on student achievement. This programme has been fundamental to the improvement in the proportion of students gaining at least five A*–C results in the GCSE from 46 per cent in 2003 to 90 per cent in 2006. Sixth form A-level results have similarly improved, with achievement now ranked in the top 10 per cent nationally. In the past four years the college has progressed from providing students with opportunities for learning to ensuring that every student successfully grasps those opportunities. The college is achieving both quality and equity! Outwood Grange has certainly fulfilled its motto of 'students first'.

School strategic planning

Strategic planning remains a key activity for the principal and staff to guide school change in the medium to long term. In past planning models, strategic planning was critically informed by changing values and purposes for education and/or changing expectations for learning at the national or local level. These influences continue for student-focused planning models, but with an emphasis on the requirements for personalised planning. This could require the construction of new curriculum and the development of new pedagogies to meet the aspirations of students. In addition, the implementation of student personalised planning, to the extent demonstrated by Lymm High School, takes time. It requires a partial school re-organisation and a shift in priorities for the deployment of resources.

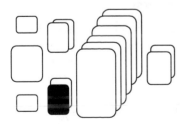

A majority of schools are now well versed in strategic planning, due to the requirements of self-management and related responsibilities and accountabilities. In the sense of re-imagining the self-managing school though, strategic planning is envisaged as including not only an outline of proposed major changes and possibilities for progressive implementation over a set period, but also the development of 'strategic intentions to guide the management of continuous and often turbulent change' (Caldwell and Spinks, 1998). Strategic planning is also envisaged as encompassing the development of major policies, initiating and undertaking research and development projects and creating strategic alliances. The student-focused school is characterised by an avid seeking of better practices to advance student learning. This requires schools to be proactive in identifying and developing promising ideas, as well as being at the forefront of innovative practice. It is not possible for schools to attempt these endeavours alone and hence the need for creating strategic alliances and participating in networks to share the effort and cost and increase the knowledge base. The Specialist Schools and Academies Trust (SSAT) has been successful in encouraging the development of networks of schools in the UK and internationally through iNet.

Strategic planning in the student-focused school is a critical activity. It can no longer be left to committees of volunteers. It now requires the distribution of leadership and a commitment of resources to ensure that it is a driving force for research and development in the school. Like student personalised planning, it requires an implementation plan to be developed on an annual basis to underpin the activity, with this plan identifying purposes, guidelines, activities, resources and evaluation strategies. This would include not only those elements of major change but also those elements and resources necessary to underpin the processes of strategic planning.

Design of and access to learning programmes

The outcome of student personalised planning and school strategic planning is the design of relevant learning programmes and planning to ensure that each student has access to those programmes uniquely suited to his/her learning targets, needs, interests, aptitudes and aspirations.

Providing a curriculum and related pedagogy that is uniquely suited to each student is no easy task, particularly within a crowded curriculum. Some schools are also constrained by the requirements of a national curriculum. Tasmania developed a new kindergarten to Year 10 curriculum around 'Essential Learnings' (Department of

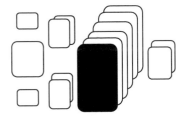

Education, Tasmania, 2002). It was designed as a response to both the crowded curriculum and the need to engage students more deeply in relevant learning, focusing on high-order thinking. The curriculum is constructed around a framework of thinking, communicating, social responsibility, personal futures and world futures. Victoria is pursuing a similar development based on a set of 'Essential Learning Standards' (VELS – Victorian Essential Learning Standards).

The Tasmanian curriculum was reviewed in 2006, when controversy arose about the language of the reform as well as approaches to assessment and reporting. However, the purpose remained intact: 'Students are learning to learn; think, know and understand; create purposeful futures; act ethically; relate, participate and care; and lead full, healthy lives' (Department of Education, Tasmania, 2006).

Providing a curriculum that is uniquely suited to each student does not mean that the curriculum for each student will be entirely different from any other. There will be many overlaps and it is still possible to group students for access to a common curriculum. The important consideration is that the timetable does not dictate curriculum possibilities for the student but that it is constructed to enable each student to access the programmes suited to his/her targets, needs, interests, aptitudes and aspirations. This approach has become the culture in many schools, especially where there is greater flexibility in curriculum construction. Technology has assisted in this development by easing the burden of constructing timetables in large complex schools. Wendy Johnson, Principal of Victor Harbor High School in South Australia, is developing an approach where the students in the one 'class' are each pursuing a different learning activity uniquely suited to the individual's needs, with the teacher being a facilitator of learning rather than a provider of learning. Many other schools in Victoria and South Australia are pursuing similar objectives through multiple learning pathways.

Providing a curriculum that is uniquely suited to each student may also require schools to create new curriculum. As indicated in an earlier section, this may well be an indicator of the degree to which a school has truly personalised student learning. On a recent visit by Jim Spinks to Reece High School in Tasmania, Principal Sheree Vertigan described the construction of a new curriculum that was required to meet the learning needs of a student with aspirations in sound engineering.

A major issue facing schools in providing curriculum uniquely suited to each student relates to time for learning. The curriculum designed to meet specific students' targets, needs, interests, aptitudes and aspirations does not necessarily fit within the confines of the standard student learning week. This is an issue of some importance to specialist schools, where the specialism can involve considerable additional time. This can be addressed by a transfer of time from the non-specialist curriculum areas, but probably not without a decrease in related attainments. An answer is to plan to use a more flexible approach to the school day, with variable lengths dependent on the requirements of individual students. This could increase the demand on resources for additional staff. Taylor and Ryan (2005) report the success of John Cabot City Technology College in Bristol in significantly adding value to student learning, and noted that extending the learning week from 25 to 30 hours was a key strategy contributing to that success.

The design of and access to learning programmes and other programmes that provide necessary support is the core business of schools. It requires exceptional leadership and management by key personnel within the school. It is usually divided up into a set of related programmes reflecting the nature of the curriculum, depending on whether the focus is on a curriculum organised as traditional learning disciplines or as an integrated set of strands, as in the Victorian Essential Learning Standards (VELS). Support programmes include administration, ICT, library and learning resources. Each programme becomes the responsibility of a leader, who works with a team of teachers and other professionals.

Programme teams are responsible for both design and delivery of programmes within the requirements of student personalised planning and the school strategic plan. This involves not only curriculum design and pedagogical development, but also the preparation of associated policies and implementation plans, including budget proposals and processes for monitoring and evaluation.

Resource planning involves the allocation of student learning time, student-focused funding and learning space availability in relation to priorities for learning both across all programmes in the school and within each programme. In this sense, the professionals who work in each programme are best equipped to prepare an implementation plan and budget. If the sum of the proposals exceeds the learning time, money and space available, then the balance can be achieved through an assessment of competing priorities in relation to the overall priorities for the school as expressed in strategic plans. The achievement of this balance requires sensitive leadership and management, particularly within schools in England where the overall school budget can include responsibility for major infrastructure development and expenditure and where significant revenue streams originate from business partnerships, philanthropic organisations and specific funding to address agreed targets.

This approach may challenge some current practice, whereby budget preparation is identified as mainly the realm of business managers. In this respect, there is a need to distinguish between creating budgets, coordinating budgets and managing budgets. Coordination and the management of budgets are best undertaken by trained specialised personnel. It is in the creation of budgets that critical input is required from those responsible for the design and delivery of student learning in relation to targets and priorities. Unfortunately resource planning has become too segmented into human resource management and financial management. These categories are a convenience for the coordination and management of the budget, but do not necessarily assist in the creation of a budget, where there is a need to consider resources in the global sense to ensure that the most effective and efficient benefit is gained in relation to student learning. Involving the same personnel in creating budgets and managing budgets can result in the preservation of the status quo and/or some 'add-ons' where some degree of abandonment is necessary. This situation is often expressed in claims of a lack of flexibility in resource deployment.

Student-focused funding allocations to schools need to take account of the changing patterns in the nature, needs, interests, aptitudes and aspirations of students and related targets for learning. Schools need to maintain flexibility to deploy resources to reflect changing patterns. The participation of all staff in their programme teams in creating resource proposals ensures that the required flexibility is at the forefront in planning. The inclusion of personalised provision, particularly for those students identified to be at risk, needs to be given some emphasis. Examples of budget planning in relation to these students are given in Chapter 9.

The student's outcomes

A planning model is incomplete without provision of processes for monitoring and evaluation, including strategic and student personalised planning and design and delivery of programmes relating to learning and teaching and their support. These processes are now common practice in most schools. However, it is also common practice to aggregate student data by class or subject and to include indicative data. Indicative data may well facilitate student learning progress, but they do not necessarily guarantee that progress has occurred or will occur. Data relating to staff professional development, student attendance and student retention are examples of indicative information.

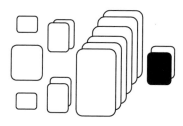

The advent of an unrelenting spotlight on student-focused outcomes in the 1990s, followed by student-focused funding and now student-focused planning, with its strong emphasis on the achievements of the individual student, means that it is now an imperative that 'the student's outcomes' provide the critical basis for evaluation and review. All planning and provision is initiated by the nature, needs, interests, aptitudes and aspirations of individual students. Review, therefore, must focus on the outcomes and achievements of each student in relation to his/her targets for learning, development and growth as a person and aspirations for learning and through learning. In England, the percentage of students achieving five good GCSE passes has served as a good indicator of the success of reforms to date, but transformation of the kind under consideration in this book also requires an indicator such as the percentage of students achieving or exceeding their personal outcome targets, with all targets being above a standard set on the basis of that required to enable a student to positively participate in society. In summary, all evaluation and review should be informed by the degree to which each student's outcomes meet expectations, as initially established and as they relate to the specific programme under review.

There will still be a need for other data, which may be indicative in nature. Such information can be valuable in proposing how programmes can be re-designed and further developed to overcome identified gaps when students do not achieve outcomes identified in personal targets.

Evaluation for improvement is but one reason for undertaking these activities. An equally, if not more, important activity is to provide data to lay the foundation for celebrations of the success of individual students in achieving targets and the overall success of the school in securing success for its students.

Evaluation and review of all programmes in relation to each student achieving personal targets is a key activity in the school. Like strategic and personalised student planning, it requires support through high-level leadership and allocation of key personnel. For this reason, it is proposed that a separate implementation plan and budget be created on an annual basis to ensure that evaluation and review is central to ongoing efforts to achieve transformation.

Developing a student-focused planning model

The model is not intended to be definitive but to illustrate an approach that recognises the student as the most important unit of organisation. Although schools have aspired to this in the past, classes or groups of students have invariably been treated as the most important unit of the organisation. The capacity to place the student at the centre is now an imperative. Transformation along these lines will be an incremental process in most schools, with the initial emphasis on students most at risk, although many schools have made remarkable progress towards re-imagining the

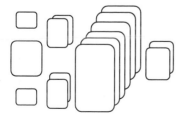

self-managing school since the beginning of the twenty-first century. This progress occurs in the context of continuous and often turbulent change.

The way forward

Progress to transformation can be assisted by a set of strategic intentions that guide the change and ensure that the ideal is not lost in the turbulence. The following points are offered for this purpose. They are not intended to be definitive or exhaustive; schools should form their own.

1   The nature, needs, interests, aptitudes and aspirations of the student provide the basis for setting targets that are realistic and achievable, shaping a planning process that will optimise learning and personal growth.

2   It is an expectation that all students will achieve a minimum standard sufficient to ensure their positive and successful participation in society.

3   Although the student's outcomes are central to the operation of the school, there still needs to be an agreed set of values, purposes and expectations with application to all students, thus ensuring coherence and harmony in the operation of the school.

4   The setting of outcome targets for each student should be paralleled by capacities to continually monitor progress and provide supportive counselling, mentoring and coaching.

5   Although the student as an individual is central to school planning, there is a need to strategically plan for overall school development, particularly in relation to where significant gaps are identified between outcome targets and achievement, and where new trends are identified that may shape the setting of new targets.

6   School priorities should be set to close unacceptable gaps between student outcome targets and achievement in particular areas of learning.

7   Curriculum and pedagogy need to be designed and delivered to ensure that the outcome targets for each student are matched by relevant learning activities. Although this provision may be made through a number of elements, they should 'jigsaw' together, with the whole possibly exceeding the sum of its parts in relation to essential learnings for the future.

8 A school may need to design new curriculum to optimise the achievement of learning potential for particular students. Sharing the overall provision for a student with other learning and teaching entities may be an option.

9 Meeting outcome targets for students requires schools to avidly seek to identify and encompass emerging better practices. Forming strategic alliances or networks with other schools or entities may assist in these processes by sharing expertise, experience and cost.

10 The deployment of resources (learning time, student-focused funding and learning space) in the best interests of students as they seek to achieve their outcome targets is central to creating school budgets. Budget planning should include demonstration of the links between planned student learning and the deployment of all resources.

11 The capacity of the school to 'value-add' to student learning is the measure of the degree to which each student exceeds his/her outcome targets set in relation to their nature, needs, interests, aptitudes and aspirations.

12 The monitoring, evaluation and review of all school programmes should be focused on the degree of achievement of related student outcome targets.

Chapter 9

Student-focused planning in action

Introduction

Personalising learning is central to success in the student-focused school. The curriculum is based on the nature, needs, interests, aptitudes and aspirations of the student for whom realistic outcomes are set. The progress and performance of each student are carefully monitored to ensure that all is on track. Counselling, coaching and mentoring are provided as required. The student-focused school also ensures that every student achieves or exceeds the minimum standards necessary for positive and successful participation in society.

The student-focused planning model in Chapter 8 provides a framework for action. It was developed from practice in schools that are succeeding in their efforts to secure success for all students, regardless of personal and socio-economic circumstance.

The purpose of Chapter 9 is to illustrate the student-focused school in action. This can be best accomplished by describing the approach as it is applied to individual students. Bridget, Joseph and Kyle have been selected as a sample. They attend different high schools or secondary colleges with features evident in both England and Australia. These descriptions do not refer to any particular person or school. The chapter concludes with a proposed budget structure that specifies allocations to support students like Bridget, Joseph and Kyle and an outline of requirements for precision in monitoring readiness and progress to guide the design of instruction on a day-by-day basis, taking up proposals in *Breakthrough* (Fullan et al., 2006) introduced in Chapters 3 and 4.

We begin with the story of Bridget, a young girl brimming with confidence, followed by the stories of Joseph and Kyle. Joseph has recently arrived as a refugee from Sudan and approaches his experience at the school with trepidation. Kyle has spent a considerable time in care and remains reluctant to commit to school, but is tempted by the possibilities.

Bridget: brimming with confidence and talent

Nature, needs, interests, aptitudes and aspirations

Bridget commenced Year 7 in 2004. In primary school she had always exceeded expectations for learning, particularly in relation to languages, thinking, learning skills and interpersonal development. Her primary school provided a bilingual programme in Japanese. Bridget had participated in this programme for six years, with half her learning time across the curriculum being undertaken in Japanese. She excelled in this learning environment and was assessed as being fluent for her age in reading, writing and speaking in Japanese. Her attainments on entry to high school are summarised in Table 9.1.

Targets for learning

Based on her attainments on entry to high school and related data on expected outcomes, the following targets were set for Bridget's high school career. Discussion with Bridget and her family was also an essential factor in the target-setting process.

- Achievement of at least ten learning area awards at A or B level in Year 10;
- Achievement of a Secondary Certificate of Education (SCE) score of 98–100 to ensure entry of her choice to any Australian university language course;
- Inclusion of two Asian languages in her learning programme throughout high school;
- Successful completion of the International Baccalaureate examinations in Year 12 to guarantee entry to international tertiary institutions, if required.

Curriculum provision

Bridget successfully sought entry to a specialist school in the study of foreign languages. The curriculum in Years 7–8 was constructed

Table 9.1 Summary of Bridget's progress report, Term 4, 2005

Progress Report Student: Bridget	Term 4 2005 Year 6
Learning Area	Rating
English – Reading	A
Writing	A
Speaking and Listening	A
Mathematics	B
Science	B
Information and Communications Technology	A
Thinking	A
Learning Skills	A
Interpersonal Development	A
Health and Physical Education	B
Civics and Citizenship	B
Society and the Environment	B
Languages (Japanese)	A+
Design, Creativity and Technology	B
The Arts	B

Ratings:
A Well above the expected standard by approximately 2 years
B Above the expected standard by approximately 1 year
C At the expected standard
D Below the expected standard
E Well below the expected standard

(Based on Victorian Essential Learning Standards (VCAA, 2005) and ratings for report cards in Victoria (DET, 2005))

around 'essential learning' strands of physical, personal and social learning; discipline-based learning and interdisciplinary learning (these are the strands in the Victorian Essential Learning Standards programme, selected here for the purposes of illustration).

Within these strands, it was possible to personalise learning in relation to targets. However, within the discipline-based learning strand, provision could only be made for Bridget to study Cantonese as a foreign language as well as address other expectations. To meet her target to study two foreign languages in each year of high school, provision was made for her to study Indonesian independently, with tutorial support of one hour per week provided by a senior language teacher. The cost of learning support materials and the tutorials was covered from the school 'specialist' budget of AU$500 per student per annum successfully undertaking a foreign language study and AU$800 per student successfully undertaking two foreign language studies (all amounts in this chapter are in Australian Dollars).

There was concern in relation to Bridget maintaining development of her fluency in Japanese. This was addressed by her participation in the school's Australia–Japan programme, including a key role in assisting in the development of the network between the schools, with conversational communication between Japanese and Australian students on the internet using Skype. By Year 8 Bridget was also conducting after school tutorials for Year 10–12 students studying Japanese.

Monitoring and support

Bridget's progress in achieving her learning targets was closely monitored by the Essential Learning Coordinator for Years 7 and 8, who monitored the learning outcomes performance data base. Her name always appeared in 'green' indicating that she was always on track to achieve her targets according to the correlations between current attainment and predicted outcomes.

Bridget's personal growth and development was monitored by her Home Group Teacher and the Home Group Coordinator for the sub-school (the school was organised as four sub-schools, each consisting of a number of home groups with students from Years 7 to 12 in each). There was always concern that Bridget's work load could be detrimental to her personal growth and development, particularly in relation to her interpersonal development and her skills in listening and responding. Ongoing counselling and support were provided to ensure that a balance of studies and personal development was maintained.

A progress report for Bridget at the completion of Year 8 is shown in Table 9.2. It should be noted that the A and B awards refer to expected standards two or one year respectively above the current year of enrolment of the student. Bridget is well on track to achieve her personal learning targets. Her current levels of attainment provide a sound basis for the construction of Years 9–10

Table 9.2 Summary of Bridget's progress report, Term 4 2007

Progress Report Student: BRIDGET		Term 4 2007 Year 8
Learning Strand	*Learning Area*	*Rating*
Physical, Personal and Social learning	Health & Physical Education	C
	Interpersonal Development	B
	Personal Learning Management	A
	Civics and Citizenship	A
Discipline-based Learning	The Arts	B
	English	A
	Society and the Environment	B
	Languages – Cantonese	B
	Languages – Indonesian	A
	Languages – Japanese	A+
	Mathematics	C
	Science	C
Interdisciplinary Learning	Communication	B
	Design, Creativity and Technology	B
	ICT	A
	Thinking	A

Ratings:
A Well above the expected standard by approximately 2 years
B Above the expected standard by approximately 1 year
C At the expected standard
D Below the expected standard
E Well below the expected standard

(Based on Victorian Essential Learning Standards (VCAA, 2005) and ratings for report cards in Victoria (DET, 2005))

curriculum and the pursuit of her aspirations for learning and through learning.

Joseph: excited but tentative

Nature, needs, interests, aptitudes and aspirations

Joseph and his family are refugees from Sudan. He is 12 but has no prior experience of school and no knowledge of English. The neighbourhood school in which Joseph is enrolling is a specialist school in ICT and language development. There are significant numbers of students from refugee families in the school. It is located in an urban area of socio-economic deprivation. Joseph's father and mother successfully sought refugee status for the family through the United Nations Commission for Refugees. As yet no family member has been successful in gaining employment.

His family has high hopes for Joseph and considers that the school is a vital part of his future. Joseph is small, well coordinated and loves games. Some interest has been expressed by his family in Joseph later transferring to a nearby specialist sports school in view of his love for and success in games.

Joseph has extreme levels of need in relation to gaining English language skills. It is also highly probable that he has extreme need in gaining basic learning skills due to his lack of prior school experience and his lack of familiarity with Australian customs and values.

Targets for learning

Apart from the eventual outcome target of at least six awards at C level (including English and mathematics) at the end of Year 10 to provide a sound basis for his senior years, it is unrealistic to set specific learning targets for Joseph at this point in time. It is more appropriate to focus on his need to gain English language and general learning skills and to pursue these goals with the maximum support possible. His learning goals should also address his need to gain an understanding of Australian customs and values. Attendance and school participation goals should also be set to assist his overall integration and valuing of learning.

Curriculum provision

A personal curriculum for Joseph is of the highest priority. He needs support from adults to build confidence and yet needs independence as a young adolescent through which to establish positive relations with his peers. He needs to maintain his Sudanese language skills and yet rapidly become literate in English. He needs to maintain his strong family relationships and yet rapidly gain an understanding and an appreciation of local customs and values.

Personalising Joseph's learning within these parameters presents a challenge. However, student-focused funding ensures that his needs can be met. Using Victoria for the purpose of illustration, a typical student-focused funding model would provide the following resources each year:

Core student learning	AU$5,800
ESL (new arrival in high Student Family Occupation (SFO) index school)	4,000
Student in a high SFO index school	500
Year 7–9 student in very high SFO index school	1,750
Total student-focused funding	AU$12,050

This amount does not have to be spent directly and entirely on Joseph, as some will be required for the overall operation of the school and to support groups of students. However, the amount is substantial and should be deployed in the best interests of student learning on a school-wide basis but with a particular focus on Joseph.

In consultation with the family, the school decided to trial the following approach to curriculum provision:

• Include Joseph in a small group of similar students in a before-school, one hour per school day language programme, commencing with breakfast and focusing intensely on spoken and written language correlated to his immediate needs to be literate in English both within the school and within the community.

• Include Joseph within the curriculum expectations for all Year 7 students to ensure his normal association with peers and to enable him to gain experience across the whole curriculum. The majority of his teachers will be experienced in working with groups of students that include recent refugees. All his classes will include other recent arrivals from Sudan. Language aide support in the classroom will be provided to Joseph on an 'as required' basis, especially when his confidence in the learning area is of concern or if there is a possible issue of safety through Joseph not being able to readily understand safety requirements. It is expected that the language aide time would diminish as his confidence and language skills develop. Aide time will then be shifted to continuing arrivals through the refugee programme.

• Build on Joseph's attributes in relation to games and coordination and keep open the later possibility of transferring to the nearby sport specialist school by immediately linking with that school's after-school development programme. This programme operates three afternoons a week and emphasises the development of skill, speed, strength, endurance, health and nutrition. The programme is partially supported by an international sports equipment manufacturer and a government agency for urban development. It is a popular programme for boys and girls of Joseph's age. As part of this support, participating students are often provided with free entry to major local and state sporting events in a supervised group. Such involvement could also assist Joseph with his understanding of local customs and values.

Monitoring and support

Joseph's progress in all learning areas will be closely monitored on a weekly basis by the Essential Learning Coordinator for Years 7 and 8. The initial emphasis will be on encouraging and rewarding any measurable progress, with the intention of assessing his potential to learn and setting achievable and short-term learning targets. Progress reports will be provided at fortnightly intervals, with the language aide ensuring understanding by the family. The progress reports will focus on success.

Joseph's progress in his personal growth and development will be closely monitored by his Home Group Teacher and his Sub-School Coordinator. Counselling will be provided on at least a weekly basis. An immediate goal will be to identify a mentor for Joseph from among the senior students in his sub-school. Coordination with the programme provided by the sports specialist school will be the responsibility of the Sub-School Coordinator. Reports on progress in Joseph's personal growth and development will be an important part of his fortnightly progress report.

Finalising the fortnightly progress report will be the responsibility of the Sub-School Coordinator, assisted by the Year 7 and 8 Essential Learning Coordinator. If progress does not occur or drops unexpectedly, then immediate action will be initiated to identify problems and provide Joseph with care and support.

Kyle: reluctant but tempted

Nature, needs, interests, aptitudes and aspirations

Kyle entered the school in April 2004 when he was 13. Most of his life has been spent in care (in several care homes) due to the frequent incarceration of his mother for substance abuse and related offences. His mother left school at 14. The whereabouts of his father is unknown and relatives have not been prepared to take responsibility for his care, although his grandmother was a strong support until her death. Prior to high school, Kyle had a very poor record of school attendance and a history of substance abuse and petty crime. He suffers from poor health and low self-esteem. School and associated learning has been a low priority for Kyle. His learning needs are a reflection of family socio-economic background, with low valuing of learning, illiteracy and rejection of many of the structures of society.

A summary of Kyle's progress report from primary school is shown in Table 9.3. It should be noted that the A to E ratings indicate the level of learning in relation to the expected standard for the year concerned, which is expressed as C. The B and A ratings are awarded in relation to the student achieving at the standard of expectation for one or two years above current year of learning, respectively. Kyle is commencing high school with exceedingly poor preparation and his prospects are far from good.

Surprisingly, Kyle has a positive outlook on life and sees his future as possibly related to the automotive industry. At least this provides a possibility around which to construct a learning programme for him that he might see as desirable and achievable.

Targets for learning

The outcome predictions based on Kyle's Year 6 attainments do not include any C level awards at the end of Year 10. For entry to an apprenticeship course at the end of Year 10, the minimum requirements are five C level awards including English, mathematics, science and ICT. This means that Kyle's learning targets have to be set above those predicted to be reasonable and achievable based on his past performance. For Kyle to achieve these targets, the school is acknowledging that it will need to add value to his learning to a very high degree.

Table 9.3 Summary of Kyle's progress report, Term 4, 2005

Progress Report Student: Kyle	Term 4 2005 Year 6
Learning Area	Rating
English – Reading	E
Writing	E
Speaking and Listening	D
Mathematics	E
Science	E
Information and Communications Technology	C
Thinking	E
Learning Skills	E
Interpersonal Development	E
Health and Physical Education	E
Civics and Citizenship	E
Society and the Environment	E
Languages	
Design, Creativity and Technology	E
The Arts	D

Ratings:
A Well above the expected standard by approximately 2 years
B Above the expected standard by approximately 1 year
C At the expected standard
D Below the expected standard
E Well below the expected standard

(Based on Victorian Essential Learning Standards (VCAA, 2005) and ratings for report cards in Victoria (DET, 2005))

Following discussion with Kyle, his carers and staff from the Department of Children's Welfare, the following outcome targets were set for Kyle:

- Fortnightly attendance target of 90 per cent;
- Nil suspensions;
- 100 per cent participation in monitoring and support sessions;
- Five subject awards at D level by the end of Year 7 including English, mathematics, science and ICT;

- Five subject awards at C level by the end of Year 8 including English, mathematics, science and ICT;
- Five subject awards at C level by the end of Year 10 including English, mathematics, science and ICT.

Curriculum provision

Providing Kyle with a curriculum to enable him to achieve these targets was a challenge. In essence he was required to accelerate his learning as well as significantly modify his behaviour and values base. The school has a very high density of high need students, with commensurate access to student-focused funding which recognises that the cost of supporting Kyle's learning would be high. Student-focused funding provided to the school in relation to Kyle is as follows.

Core student learning (Year 7–8)	AU$5,800
Student in a high SFO index school	500
Year 7–9 student in very high SFO index school	1,750
Year 7–8 student identified at exceptional risk	3,000
Total student-focused funding	AU$11,050

It was considered imperative for Kyle to have access to a comprehensive curriculum that covers all the essentials for learning now and in the future. However, this did not allow sufficient learning time to be devoted to accelerating his learning to the required degree, particularly in literacy and numeracy. It was decided to extend his school day by one hour prior to the beginning of the day and to use this additional time to focus on nutrition, presentation, literacy and numeracy, with the learning geared to assisting with his normal school curriculum. For this before-school session, Kyle joined a group of six other boys needing to accelerate their learning.

The school also recognised the likelihood of Kyle experiencing real difficulties in his transition to high school, particularly in his first year where the temptation to return to school avoidance would be strong. To increase support to cover this possibility, it was decided to include Kyle in an industry outreach programme providing mentoring to high risk students. The programme is partially supported by an automotive manufacturer, but required deployment of some student-focused funding to ensure that Kyle had access to his mentor for at least three hours per week after school. The mentor provided by the programme had the capacity to tutor as well as provide support to help Kyle overcome obstacles to successful school attendance and participation.

Monitoring and support

Kyle's progress in all learning areas was closely monitored on a weekly basis by the Essential Learning Coordinator for Years 7 and 8. The initial emphasis was on encouraging and rewarding any measurable progress, including gains from his before-school acceleration programme. Reports were provided at fortnightly intervals.

Kyle's progress in his personal growth and development was closely monitored by his Home Group Teacher and his Sub-School Coordinator. Counselling occurred on at least a weekly basis. Close contact was maintained with Kyle's mentor to gain further insights that might assist his development, and to alert school staff to any known out-of-school factors that might impede his development.

Finalising the fortnightly progress report was the responsibility of the Sub-School Coordinator, assisted by the Years 7 and 8 Essential Learning Coordinator. If progress did not occur or dropped unexpectedly, then immediate action was initiated to identify problems and provide Kyle with additional care and support.

After a shaky start, Kyle successfully adapted to the school learning environment. He thoroughly tested the school position of never giving up on any student. His mentor was very important in supporting him through the early period, particularly in relation to connecting the satisfaction of overcoming difficulties in learning with the possible later rewards of an apprenticeship leading to employment. His progress report is summarised in Table 9.4.

Kyle successfully achieved his learning and personal targets for the end of Year 8. Attendance was 92 per cent with no suspensions. Seven awards at C level had been achieved, including the necessary English, mathematics, science and ICT. As the predicted outcome based on Year 6 attainment was zero awards at level C, the school had added considerable value. As well, he had remained with the same care family for 2004 and 2005 and re-established connections with his mother. His Sub-School Coordinator arranged for Kyle's mother to receive copies of his fortnightly progress reports. She is now looking forward to her own future on release from prison, with

Table 9.4 Summary of Kyle's progress report, Term 4, 2007

Progress Report Student: KYLE		Term 4 2007 Year 8
Learning Strand	*Learning Area*	*Rating*
Physical, Personal and Social Learning	Health and Physical Education	C
	Interpersonal Development	D
	Personal Learning Management	C
	Civics and Citizenship	D
Discipline-based Learning	The Arts	E
	English	C
	Society and the Environment	E
	Languages	
	Mathematics	C
	Science	C
Interdisciplinary Learning	Communication	D
	Design, Creativity and Technology	C
	ICT	C
	Thinking	D

Ratings:
A Well above the expected standard by approximately 2 years
B Above the expected standard by approximately 1 year
C At the expected standard
D Below the expected standard
E Well below the expected standard

(Based on Victorian Essential Learning Standards (VCAA, 2005) and ratings for report cards in Victoria (DET, 2005))

Kyle's continuing progress in learning at school as central to that future.

Kyle is now ready to proceed to Year 9 with his end of Year 10 targets well in sight. Although his learning acceleration was impressive, it was successfully argued that he was still 'a student at high risk'. This enables the 'student high risk' additional funding of AU$3,000 per annum to be retained to support Kyle's continuation in the mentoring programme, with expansion to include onsite workplace experience in an automotive plant for the Friday of each school week.

This means a diminution of time in some learning areas. Monitoring and reporting is being maintained at previous levels, with provision for a return to before-school tutoring should Kyle become at risk of faltering on the way to achieving his subject target levels.

Saving Kyle: a 'default position'

In a presentation at the 14th National Conference of the Specialist Schools and Academies Trust in November 2006, Sir Dexter Hutt, Executive Headteacher of Ninestiles Community School, Birmingham related the 'Saving of Corey' – a story of personalising the learning of a young lad remarkably similar in background to Kyle. After years of struggle, support, intervention, laughter, despair and celebration, Corey successfully completed secondary education at Ninestiles and is now a positive and thriving participant in the wider community.

Hutt remarked that it is not unusual for a Corey to be saved in a twentieth-century school, but that it is certainly not the 'default position', with a guarantee that all students from sad and dysfunctional backgrounds will successfully complete school and use education as a launching pad for positive participation in the world at large. All schools are only too aware of the many Kyles and Coreys who fall through even the best safety nets.

In proposing a characteristic of the twenty-first-century school, Hutt challenged his audience to regard the saving of the Kyles and the Coreys as the 'default position'. In the twentieth-century school this would be but a hope. However, success for all students in all settings is possible with current advances in personalising learning, including the capacity to set targets, design and deliver learning and teaching of the highest quality, carefully and intensively monitor progress, positively intervene where necessary, and preparedness to judge schools on the outcomes.

It is certain that former Prime Minister Tony Blair would support the default position for the twenty-first century schools proposed by Sir Dexter Hutt. In his Prime Ministerial address to the 14th National Conference of the Specialist Schools and Academies Trust in November 2006, he challenged headteachers and all educators in a concluding statement:

> The vision is clear: a state sector that has independent, non-fee-paying schools which remain utterly true to the principle of

educating all children, whatever their background or ability, to the highest possible level . . . With your leadership and example, we now have a once-in-a-generation opportunity to forge a national consensus around this vision. You who have done so much to change education in Britain for the better, are those who can translate that vision into practice.

(Blair, 2006b)

A 're-imagined school' for Bridget, Joseph and Kyle

Leading-edge schools in Australia, England and many other countries are successfully 're-imagining the self-managing school' to the benefit of students. They characteristically sustain their success in adding significant value to student learning outcomes. Bridget, Joseph and Kyle, along with their school colleagues, are enjoying the benefits. As these schools are student focused, it is appropriate to identify their characteristics through the eyes of students as a way of summarising what has been presented thus far in Chapter 9.

'In my school . . .'

'The principal/headteacher knows my name and always speaks to me.'

'All staff smile and listen during conversations with me.'

'Everyone is as concerned about my welfare and wellbeing as they are with the achievement of my learning outcome targets.'

'My parents/carers think my school is fantastic.'

'All my friends have personal learning targets that they see as challenging but achievable. I certainly like mine.'

'I feel that my teachers trust me to make good choices about what and how I learn.'

'Staff do not give up on me if I make mistakes or fall down on expectations. Instead they encourage and support me to try again.'

'All my friends love their learning programmes. No one has classes that they hate. All my teachers are very enthusiastic about our work.'

'We have very few students who misbehave in class, as we all enjoy our learning and want to make good progress.'

'The school has superb resources to support our learning. Laptops and musical instruments are even available for those students without home computers or their own musical instruments.'

'We can use the school laptops anywhere within the school buildings using the wireless network. We can even link our own laptops into the network.'

'I can often use school resources and sports facilities after school.'

'I often link to students in other schools and countries who share my learning interests.'

'Everyone is pleased when I do well and it feels good to be congratulated.'

'My Sub-School Coordinator and Home Group Teacher are really supportive and interested in everything I do.'

'My Year Group Coordinator is fantastic in telling me if all my learning targets are on track and finding extra help when there is some slippage.'

'My school is always in the news. All students seem to perform very well and this often receives positive comment.'

'There are many opportunities to play sport and become involved in other activities with my friends.'

'I love going to school with my friends. Missing school days is not on my agenda.'

Budget structure

What would be the structure of a school budget with full implementation of student-focused planning and personalised learning? Would it be different from the structure of the past, when the unit of organisation was the school or classroom rather than the student? Can it explicitly address the resources to support students like Bridget, Joseph and Kyle?

We have searched for evidence of change in the structure of school budgets as the concepts of student-focused planning and personalising learning have developed in recent years. To date, no significant structural changes have been found. This is surprising, as student-focused allocation of resources to schools and increasing personalising of learning requires a different approach to the deployment of resources to meet the specific learning needs of individual students. It follows that the planning and tracking of such deployment would be enhanced if it was readily identifiable in the school budget.

There seem to be constraints associated with the inflexibility of current school accounting systems or the fact that personalising learning has yet to develop to the extent of encompassing all of the elements of need identification, target setting, monitoring, individualised curriculum design and delivery, monitoring and evaluation for all students. Planning at this level of detail for every student is a very large task for a school and, at most, schools appear to be only attempting this for those students known to be at risk. In this context, can a budget structure be developed that would assist schools to allocate and track expenditure for all students?

The following budget structure is proposed for consideration by those schools endeavouring to more carefully align resource deployment with the personalising of learning. It is designed to take account of the very high importance placed on the processes of planning for personalising learning, strategic planning and evaluation and review, as outlined in the model for student-focused planning in Chapter 8.

It is proposed that the school budget be structured around the following headings:

Student Personalised Planning
Strategic Planning
Leadership and Administration
Learning Programmes
Individual Intervention
Learning Support
Evaluation and Review
Premises, Grounds and Utilities.

Preparation of the Student Personalised Planning, Strategic Planning and Evaluation and Review budgets has been described in the associated sections in the student-focused planning model in Chapter 8. The Leadership and Administration and Premises, Grounds and Utilities components are self-explanatory. Learning Support includes library, ICT and any other support to learning programmes.

Learning programmes may vary in number and type, depending on the nature of the curriculum. It is through these programmes that curriculum is designed and delivered to students. In the past, students chose from a standard curriculum but, with personalising learning, there is the possibility that curriculum may have to be 'created' to meet the aspiration of students for learning and through learning.

In Victoria, learning programmes would normally be related to the Victorian Essential Learning Standards (VELS), as illustrated in the proposed student-focused planning model. This would entail the preparation of plans and budgets to design and deliver curriculum in the domains of physical, personal and social learning; discipline-based learning and interdisciplinary learning. Larger schools may well subdivide each strand into its composite strands for planning purposes. In England, learning programmes are more likely to relate to the ten key areas of the national curriculum.

In the past these programmes have provided comprehensive coverage for planning and budgeting. But do they sufficiently cover those students where extraordinary provision and support needs to be made to ensure that learning is optimised and learning targets met? Planning for this provision can be made through the Individual Intervention Programme, which covers provision for individual students above and beyond the standard learning programmes. This type of provision is illustrated in the proposed student-focused planning model as it was applied for Bridget, Joseph and Kyle in the first part of this chapter. It particularly relates to situations where the length of the 'learning week' is extended or intensive tutoring or mentoring are provided to overcome learning impediments. Planning should include provision for cases known at the commencement of the year, as well as estimation of possible requirements that may emerge as the year proceeds.

For each of the above planning and budgeting components, it is proposed that initial estimates should be provided by the team responsible for design and delivery of the programme. Plans and estimates should follow an agreed format to facilitate within-school comparisons and refinements. It is suggested that each programme plan should include the following:

- name of programme
- programme purpose
- outcome targets
- planning elements, including costs for personnel and materials
- performance monitoring
- evaluation and review.

Plans of this nature need not be lengthy. Many schools already use similar mechanisms and limit each programme plan to two typed pages. Elements of the plan include short descriptions of how learning or support is to occur, with estimates of the associated costs of personnel, materials, travel and so on. For the Individual Intervention Programme, each student should be represented as a separate planning element.

Planning may well reveal a need to more closely align the 'teaching' with the intended 'learning', and this requires a talent force approach to ensure that the right mix of knowledge and skill is readily available to optimise outcomes for all students, irrespective of background and circumstances. In essence, planning to maximise intellectual capital is a necessity if there is to be success for all students.

Programme plans and budgets provide the estimates for developing the overall school budget. These may well initially exceed available funds, with a balanced budget being achieved through reference to the priorities expressed in the strategic plan and the overall targets for student learning. In balancing the overall school budget, it is also necessary to be cognisant of the totality of resources available to the school, including those provided by the wider community. 'Balancing the budget' is total alignment of student learning outcome expectations, not only with financial resources but also the social, intellectual and spiritual capital available to the school.

It is emphasised that the suggested approach to school budgeting is not a pure approach to the resourcing of learning that is personalised, but it incorporates an Individual Intervention Programme to accommodate the associated cost of the extraordinary provision some students require if their learning is to be optimised and good outcomes are to be achieved. The search for an ideal approach continues, where a personalised learning plan and budget is generated for every student.

Precision in monitoring readiness and progress in student achievement

Central to success in implementing the student-focused planning model is a capacity for monitoring the readiness and progress of students to assist teachers and those who support them in the design and delivery of appropriate programmes of instruction. Such a capacity was a feature in the studies of Bridget, Joseph and Kyle. A key issue is the extent to which schools have a capacity to provide data and teachers have the capacity, including time and know-how, to utilise them (see Matters, 2006 for a comprehensive account of issues related to the use of data to support learning and teaching in schools).

In Chapter 3 we described the work of Michael Fullan, Peter Hill and Carmel Crévola in *Breakthrough*. They proposed a system to lift the performance of schools. There are three components: personalisation, professional learning and precision. 'The glue that binds these three is moral purpose: education for all that raises the bar as it closes the gap' (Fullan et al., 2006, p. 16). The consistency between these components and the model for alignment and broad themes of this book is evident.

Of particular interest at this point is the concept of 'precision', as it applies to the gathering and utilisation of data. Fullan, Hill and Crévola contend that a breakthrough will be achieved only when 'classroom instruction in which the current sporadic data collection is streamlined, analysis is automated, and individualised instruction is delivered on a daily basis in every classroom' (p. 20). There are four 'ingredients' in such an approach:

1   A set of powerful and aligned assessment tools, tied to the learning objectives of each lesson, that gives the teacher access to accurate and comprehensive information on the progress of each student on a daily basis;
2   A method of allowing the formal assessment data to be captured in a way that is not time consuming;
3   A means of using the assessment information on each student to design and implement personalised instruction;
4   A built-in means of monitoring and managing learning.
    (Adapted from Fullan et al., 2006, pp. 36–7)

While they acknowledge the limitations of a transfer of practice, Fullan, Hill and Crévola draw from the field of health care to propose Critical Learning Instructional Paths (CLIPs) for each student. They demonstrate how CLIPs, combined with assessments with the above ingredients, can be applied (Fullan et al., 2006, Chapter 5). Their work continues in the design of the software programmes to support such an approach. The outcome and similar work by others in respect to 'assessment for learning' will form part of 'next practice'.

Some school systems have already made a start. An example is Catholic Education in the Archdiocese of Melbourne that has created three portals to assist schools set priorities and implement programmes on a school, class and student basis (Myinternet, Myclasses and Myportfolio). It is noteworthy that a substantial part of the foundation for *Breakthrough* was laid by Catholic Education in Melbourne. Carmel Crévola and Peter Hill led the Children's Literacy Success Strategy (CLaSS) project for Catholic Education in Melbourne, in which more than 300 schools have participated since 1998. CLaSS was shaped in part by a model for alignment of standards and targets; monitoring and assessment; classroom teaching programmes; professional learning teams; school and class organisation; intervention and special assistance; home, school and community partnerships; and leadership and organisation, with the focus and integrating force being beliefs and understandings about teaching and learning (Hill and Crévola, 2000, p. 123).

A noteworthy but informal indicator of the growing interest in precision in the use of data, as described above, may be observed in the exhibition areas of large conferences in England, where assessment for learning is one of nine 'gateways' to personalising learning (Hargreaves, 2004; 2006; Sims, 2006). We have attended the annual conference of the Specialist Schools and Academies Trust in recent years. It attracts nearly 2,000 school leaders and is supported by an exhibition (trade) area with more than 200 exhibitors. Until the early 2000s, most exhibitors displayed books and other print materials of various kinds. From about 2005, the majority have exhibited computer-based programmes that assist the gathering, interpretation and utilisation of data of one kind or another, much of which is student focused.

The way forward

This chapter illustrated what has hitherto been considered impossible in schools organised along traditional lines, namely that there can be individual learning plans for students whose nature, needs, interests, aptitudes and aspirations cover the gamut of possibilities and, even more, that a budget for the school can be assembled on the basis of such plans. Student-focused planning and budgeting along these lines is rare, and it will be a significant achievement if the majority of schools can build their capacity to do this by the end of the decade. However, the way forward must be guided by an even more demanding challenge along the lines advocated by Fullan,

Hill and Crévola (2006), namely, to work out Critical Learning Instructional Paths for each student in an educational counterpart to emerging practice in health, and ensure that there is parallel precision in assessment.

Studies of success

Introduction

The four sources of capital which are central to success should be aligned in pursuit of significant, systematic and sustained change that secures success for all students in all settings. The complexity of the task means that more attention must be given than ever before to the matter of governance. It is not just a simple process of decision-making in a school closed off from its community. These were the major themes in preceding chapters.

Chapter 10 provides examples of successful alignment in five schools. Three are from Australia (Australian Science and Mathematics School in South Australia, Glen Waverley Secondary College in Victoria and St Monica's Parish Primary School in the Australian Capital Territory), one is from a commune (municipality) in Chile (Maria Louisa Bombal School in Vitacura, Santiago) and one is from a local authority in England (Park High School in the London Borough of Harrow). A recurring feature in these studies is the importance of facilities that align with curriculum and pedagogy, and we explore this theme before telling the five stories of success.

School design as symbol and substance in alignment for transformation

There is a trend in curriculum to complement traditional discipline-based learning with interdisciplinary learning and to provide students with multiple pathways through a rich range of offerings to enable them to complete secondary school, taking account of their needs, interests, aptitudes and aspirations. Developments in curriculum are matched by developments in pedagogy that focus on personalised learning and 'learning to learn'. In England, where the concepts have been widely embraced and an increasing number of schools can justifiably lay claim to their practice, it has been helpful to conceive of personalising learning as a journey through nine interconnected 'gateways': curriculum, workforce development, school organisation and design, student voice, mentoring, learning to learn, assessment for learning, new technologies and advice and guidance (Hargreaves, 2004).

Key elements of these developments in curriculum and pedagogy can only be delivered with difficulty in traditional classroom settings, given their standard size, lack of flexibility and a configuration that is not conducive to intensive use of new technologies. This presents the challenge of replacing or refurbishing much of the learning space where these developments are a priority. It is important to note that this is the primary reason for major change. Another reason is the run-down condition of many schools. Both reasons explain a world-wide surge of interest in school design suited to the century and the upgrading where possible of existing facilities. Noteworthy are commitments in England in the Building Schools for the Future programme in which 90 per cent of space in secondary schools will be rebuilt or refurbished, and the intention in Victoria to do the same for all of its more than 1,600 state schools.

Such developments assume a connection between school design and learning outcomes. Research is sparse. Underpinning the commitment in England are two studies conducted for the Department for Education and Skills (DfES) by PricewaterhouseCoopers (PwC). The first was published in 2000 and it found 'qualitative evidence and some quantitative evidence to support the view that a positive and significant association existed between schools capital investment and student performance' (PricewaterhouseCoopers, 2003, p. i). The second, published in 2003, was more fine-grained, distinguishing between different kinds of investment. Data were drawn from 900 schools. Quantitative evidence confirmed the connection between level of investment and performance in community primary schools, and for investment in curriculum-related projects such as those related to ICT and science. Qualitative evidence confirmed a connection between level of investment and the extent to which the community in low socio-economic settings made use of school buildings. Teacher and student morale improved when investment was related to the curriculum and to the improvement of run-down facilities. Principals in very low socio-economic settings doubted that

capital investment on its own could help improve student performance, given the significance of family-related factors (these findings
drawn from PricewaterhouseCoopers, 2003).

In one the most significant studies of its kind, Bunting (2005)
highlighted the importance of facilities and likely and desired directions for their design in the future. He conducted a rigorous investi-
gation that sought the views of 23 architects and 23 educators who
were leaders in their respective fields. They were based in Australia,
Hong Kong, New Zealand and the United States. He engaged these
experts in the exploration of societal and educational factors that will
influence the design of secondary schools in the twenty-first century.
Three rounds of questions were posed, the first to secure answers to
ten sub-questions, the second to seek ratings of the desirability of
occurrence, and the third to seek ratings of probability of occurrence.
Participants could confirm or change their ratings in the light of
their knowledge of the ratings of fellow participants in previous
rounds and further developments in the field.

Bunting found that 'developments in transport and communications technology have severed the nexus between space, place and
time – the foundations of traditional architecture'. This calls into
question 'the need to attend school in the traditional way'. Moreover,
he found that 'people were desirous of a re-conceived sense of community'. Developments in curriculum and alternative forms of learning were described. He concluded that the 'need for secondary
schools needs to be re-conceptualised'. Recommendations included 'a
re-examination of the provision of secondary schools to foster their
greater relevance, and use as elements of community infrastructure'
and 'consideration of the concept of learning centres as opposed to
secondary schools'. He referred to the importance of all students
remaining in secondary schools for as long as possible, something
that requires that all experience success to get to this point. Schools
should be social as well as educational places: 'the places of learning
must be conducive to learning and congregating' (these excerpts
from Bunting, 2005, pp. ii-iv).

The OECD has published three reports on outstanding educational designs at all levels, including pre-school and tertiary, with
an expert panel assessing nominations of schools in member nations.
For the third report (OECD, 2006, p. 8) the panel employed five
criteria: flexibility, community needs, sustainability, safety and security, and alternative financing. The first, flexibility, sought designs
that were closely aligned with trends in curriculum and pedagogy:

buildings or grounds that are adapted to new forms of learning and research; institutions that make special use of information and communications technology; or special educational facilities. Characteristics include transformable learning spaces, student-centredness, problem-based learning facilities, or provision for students with physical, learning or behavioural difficulties or for 'at-risk' students.

The criterion for community needs was concerned with 'institutions that encourage community involvement and/or access by giving multiple stakeholders the opportunity to participate in their design, planning, or day-to-day management; by catering to lifelong learning; or by sharing the facilities with students' families or others'. Sustainability was concerned with 'facilities that demonstrate consideration for the environment through the efficient use of energy, choice of materials, local or natural resources, siting or management'. Alternative financing included the use of private financing or 'buildings where life-cycle costs are sustainable'. Sixty-five institutions were selected for inclusion in the report. Each met at least one of the criteria. They could be either newly built or renovated facilities.

It is evident that there is a high degree of alignment of these criteria, not only in matters related to curriculum and pedagogy, but also with prevailing or emerging values in relation to links with the community (social capital) and sustainability.

Australian Science and Mathematics School (ASMS) in South Australia

Included in the OECD report was the Australian Science and Mathematics School (ASMS) in Adelaide (South Australia), a specialist non-selective school on the site of and enjoying a close association with Flinders University. Opened in 2003, it was nominated for the OECD project on the criteria of flexibility and sustainability. The citation in the OECD report (2006, p. 130) included the following observations:

> The design of the school's learning and physical environment is based on pivotal beliefs about student-centred teaching and learning, lifelong learning, the relevance of science and mathematics to the world's future, the interconnectedness of

knowledge, and the importance of human communication in all
its forms.

The building itself is considered a 'learning tool' in 'sustainable
design and intelligent building concepts'. The working spaces of
students and teachers are known as 'commons' or 'studios':

> Each student has his or her own 'home-base' work station located
> in one of the learning commons, and the studios are fitted out
> with specialist services and hands-on facilities to enable students
> to undertake practical work and experiments which support
> activities in the learning commons.'

Brian Caldwell visited the school and saw the space utilised in the
manner described above. In one component of the programme, students are engaged in projects in which they explore critical questions
over a number of weeks, prepare reports and make presentations
to other students and teachers. There is a relaxed yet purposeful
atmosphere. The school is carpeted throughout and graffiti has never
been a problem. Teachers have a tutor role, providing support for
12–14 students with whom they spend 40 minutes every day.
Tutors receive and read every piece of work completed by students
in their group, after it has been assessed by the subject teacher.
These are good indicators of personalised learning. There were about
260 students in 2006, still under the capacity of 400, with students
coming from about 65 schools in and around Adelaide. Some come
from other states or from overseas. There are 26 teachers on the staff.
The school is immediately adjacent to the School of Education at
Flinders University, enabling it to serve as a 'laboratory' for the
latter. There is also strong collaboration with academic and research
staff in science and mathematics at the university (the concept of the
ASMS originated with academic staff at Flinders).

There is powerful alignment of curriculum, pedagogy, professional
roles, professional learning, school design and values in relation to
personalised learning and sustainability. There is misalignment to
the extent that resources are not allocated to the school in a manner
consistent with the student being the key unit of organisation and
the school being organised around tutor groups in learning commons
or studios rather than formal classrooms. Staff are allocated to the
school on the same basis as all other schools, with the addition of
three teachers because the school serves as a centre for professional

development for the school system. Cash allocations to the school from the Department of Education and Children's Services (DECS) are made on the same system-wide basis. The school supplements its income through fees charged to the large number of visitors who seek to learn about the school. Staff are appointed to the school on the basis of application to the ASMS. Applicants are aware of the curriculum and pedagogy and are normally fully committed to the vision of the school. Intellectual capital is addressed, with each member of staff having an Individual Professional Development Plan. Nine of 26 members of staff are pursuing higher degrees. Principal Jim Davies (who serves as adjunct professor at Flinders), Deputy Principal Graeme Oliver and Assistant Principal Jayne Heath contribute on a regular basis to conferences and publications. Links with business and industry are modest but increasing. Governance arrangements are similar to other schools in a government system that has limited school self-management, although the governing council has a standing sub-committee that has a key role of monitoring and supporting the partnership between the school and Flinders University.

The school has links with specialist schools in other places, notably the NUS School of Science and Mathematics in Singapore, attached to the National University of Singapore, also cited in the OECD report for its innovative design on the same criteria (flexibility and sustainability). The ASMS is an active participant in iNet (International Networking for Educational Transformation) of the London-based Specialist Schools and Academies Trust. It is seeking international accreditation for its programmes.

Glen Waverley Secondary College (GWSC) in Victoria

Glen Waverley Secondary College (GWSC) is a Years 7 to 12 secondary school with about 1,900 students in an eastern suburb of Melbourne, Australia. It serves a medium to high socio-economic community and attracts about 50 students from other countries. It is an example of a school that has changed in barely a decade from one that offered a more-or-less traditional approach to schooling in a traditional mid-twentieth-century setting to one that is technology rich and provides a curriculum, and especially a pedagogy, that is personalised, with a focus on learning to learn. The concept of 'powerful learning' has been adopted for students and staff alike, and a particular element that warrants its inclusion is the manner in which the intellectual capital of its staff has been developed and maintained. The change is now deeply embedded in the culture of the school, suggesting that it has the major features of transformation as defined in this book, especially being change that is 'significant, systematic and sustained'.

It was apparent as the changes got underway that there was a misalignment of curriculum and pedagogy on the one hand and the design of the school buildings on the other. A staged re-building programme was enabled by government grants and locally-raised funds and most of the facilities may now be considered state of the art. Many of the old buildings have been bulldozed.

There have been three principals over this period, but a coherent and compelling vision has been sustained. In each instance succession came from within the school. The second of these principals, Darrell Fraser, was appointed towards the end of the decade of development as Deputy Secretary (Schools) in the Department of Education and Training (DET) with responsibility for the system-wide development of government (state) schools in Victoria. Two members of his senior leadership team at GWSC have joined him at DET, ensuring a degree of system alignment with what transpired at Glen Waverley.

There are some features in common with the Australian Science and Mathematics School, especially in regard to pedagogy and some aspects of the new facilities, although GWSC is a comprehensive high school that opened in 1960 but was transformed from twentieth-century to twenty-first-century schooling by 2006, whereas ASMS is a specialist school in science and mathematics that was purpose built on a green-field site in 2003. There is, however, an informal partnership between the two schools. GWSC was selected by OECD as model of impact of ICT on the quality of learning and a report was prepared (Toomey and Associates, 2000). As noted in the previous section, ASMS was selected by OECD for exemplary school design (OECD, 2006).

GWSC is an interesting example of continuity and change across two governments. The Kennett Liberal National Coalition Government (1992–1999) was conservative in many respects, but radical in the changes it made to the system of government (state) schools. Government schools were previously self-managing to a modest degree but, under an initiative known as Schools of the Future, more than 90 per cent of the state's education budget was decentralised to schools for local decision-making. State-wide curriculum and standards frameworks were introduced, along with standardised tests in basic subjects in primary and early years of secondary. A performance appraisal system was introduced for teachers and principals. ICT was implemented on an unprecedented scale. Victoria was in financial crisis at the start of this period and this, combined with sharply declining enrolments in many schools, led to the closure of nearly 300 of the about 1,900 schools, with most of the affected secondary schools amalgamating with others.

Glen Waverley Secondary College seized the opportunities created by Schools of the Future. As noted in the OECD report: 'Schools of the Future has been a crucial and enabling feature of the whole school change which has taken place at GWSC. It has provided financial flexibility and freedom to determine a vision and to be able to put in place the components to realise this vision. And at the same time it has provided an accountability framework' (Toomey and Associates, 2000, p. 42). The school became a 'system leader', in the sense that it was selected as a site for the extensive introduction of ICT. It was designated as a 'Navigator School', serving as a centre for professional development for other schools in the introduction of technology. This leadership continues. The school was also part of the closure and amalgamation programme, with two nearby schools experiencing dramatic decline in enrolments closing and agreeing to amalgamate and re-locate to the site of GWSC.

The Kennett Government was defeated in the election of 1999 and replaced by the Bracks Labor Government, re-elected for a third term in 2006. The new government abandoned the terminology but maintained and, in some instances, extended the features of Schools of the Future. Once again, GWSC seized the opportunities that were created and assumed an even more significant role as a system leader, with its principal and two members of its leadership team assuming system-wide roles, as described above. The government prepared a comprehensive and coherent strategy under the title of *The Blueprint for Government Schools* (Department of Education and Training, 2003), much of which has been implemented. Its features are evident in the continuing transformation at GWSC. As noted in the school's successful submission for support from the Leading Schools Fund:

> In 2003, the Boston Consulting Report, the research that underpinned the Ministerial Blueprint, contended that there exists in the Victorian system no example of a transformed school. The report did, however, identify pockets of transformed

practice in a number of schools. One of these schools was Glen Waverley Secondary College. The journey the College embarked on nearly a decade ago has generated innovation that has attracted international attention. It spawned a learning culture capable of sustaining a first generation of change in teaching and learning practice that has delivered highly impressive outcomes. More importantly, however, it has established the preconditions necessary to support a second generation of change – transformational change.

> (GWSC, Leading Schools Fund Submission, p. 4)

Examination of the academic achievements of students, the reports of professional development of staff, interviews with students and senior staff and observation of the new facilities in action confirm the statements set out above. The school achieves at a higher level than 'like schools' (those with a similar socio-economic profile) and on a par with the often more highly profiled non-government (private) schools in similar settings. Students undertake individual projects that are triggered by 'rich questions'. An example explained to Brian Caldwell by students on one of his visits was concerned with sustainability, with participants examining ways to save paper, the findings of which are of immediate benefit to the school. The concept of sustainability is embedded in the vision and values of GWSC. As noted above, leadership sustainability is evident.

The school has a Teacher Learning Improvement Plan that offers a remarkable array of professional development opportunities including mentoring, conference participation, informal professional exchange, in-house professional development, team teaching, self-directed learning and reading, action research, learning area forums and participation in school-based practice teaching. The programme for leadership development is particularly impressive and this is closely integrated with the cycle of activities for school development. Leadership retreats are a feature. These are now embedded in the life of the school (culture) and leaders recounted a number of rituals associated with the induction of staff and the conduct of meetings (symbols), illustrating cultural and symbolic leadership in the Sergiovanni formulation (Sergiovanni, 1984). In addition to Thomas Sergiovanni, the school draws extensively from the work of international scholars including Richard Elmore, Daniel Goleman, David Perkins and Peter Senge from the USA; Michael Fullan from Canada and Guy Claxton from the UK. Australian scholar Hedley Beare helped energise the commitment to transformation in the mid-1990s and highly-regarded Australian education consultant Julia Atkin is a valued facilitator of professional development.

Except for special purpose grants that have been secured from time to time and a relatively high level of locally-raised funds, the school is funded on the same basis as like schools under Victoria's system of needs-based funding for self-managing schools. Its governance arrangements are also similar, with a school council on which parents form a majority. Partnerships with and support from others follow a general pattern for schools in Victoria, with the social capital of such schools generally weaker than their counterparts in England.

In summary, Glen Waverley Secondary College is characterised by powerful alignment of spiritual, intellectual and financial capital focused on a coherent vision for learning, with the student at the centre. It is a vision that has been sustained for more than a decade, with alignment strengthened by the design of new facilities. The school should be considered a model of sustainable leadership. There has been strong alignment with the policies of successive governments and the school and its leaders have become system leaders, in both traditional and contemporary senses of the term.

St Monica's Parish Primary School in the Australian Capital Territory

St Monica's Parish Primary School is a non-government, Catholic school in Canberra, Australian Capital Territory, that serves about 450 students from Kindergarten to Year 6. It serves a mid-range socio-economic community. In 2006, St Monica's was recognised by Teaching Australia for Excellence in School Improvement (Teaching Australia is a national organisation funded by the Australian Government that supports and presents awards for quality in teaching and school leadership). St Monica's is in the system administered by the Catholic Education Office (CEO) in the Canberra-Goulburn Diocese.

The principal of St Monica's, Mary Dorrian, was appointed in 2003. In the first year of her leadership, the school implemented an improvement programme based on the Innovative Designs for Enhancing Achievements in Schools project (IDEAS), funded by the Australian Government's Quality Teaching Programme. IDEAS is a research-based school development initiative that resulted from a partnership of the University of Southern Queensland (USQ) and Education Queensland. The research and development team was led by Professor Frank Crowther, former dean of education at USQ. The centre-piece in IDEAS is a model that has much in common with that adopted in this book, as described in Chapter 3. Alignment is sought between school-wide pedagogy (intellectual capital), cohesive community (social capital), strategic foundations (spiritual capital) and infrastructure design. The integrating mechanism is powerful professional support (intellectual capital).

St Monica's was one of the first Catholic schools to adopt IDEAS, which the school board has used since 2003 to assist with strategic planning. Mary Dorrian believes the approach was the key to success in a number of initiatives, including a literacy strategy which describes anticipated outcomes for students at all levels, supported by integrated curriculum planning. The success of the literacy programme may be seen in national literacy testing in Year 3, where 77 per cent of students from St Monica's were ranked in the two highest skill bands for reading.

St Monica's literacy strategy was also informed by research on early literacy and literacy interventions by New Zealand's Professor Dame Marie Clay. Training was provided to staff to introduce a Reading Recovery programme to assist students from Kindergarten to Year 2 who were having difficulty achieving the literacy outcomes for their level.

Professional development for all staff has been a priority for St Monica's. This is provided by education consultants from the CEO and an independent consultant engaged by the school since 2003. According to the school's citation in the 2006 Australian National Awards for Quality Schooling, 'staff have undertaken significant pedagogical change that has resulted in improved literacy results, and students developing and practising the skills to be creative researchers of the future'. The total costs of professional development exceed AU$30,000 each year and this covers consultants and relief teachers to enable staff to meet in groups for a half-day on four occasions each year. Support and training has also been given to non-teaching staff.

In addition to fostering academic, social and personal qualities, St Monica's promotes the development of spiritual (Catholic) values within its student body. Every term the entire school focuses on a key concept, which is highlighted through the teaching of two related values. Examples include 'doing our best', honesty, the environment and community.

St Monica's networks with a range of schools and community

organisations. It has a strong relationship with the parish community and welcomes the use of school facilities for parish functions. The Canberra-Goulburn CEO has established a loose network and system of support for about 50 Catholic schools in the diocese. A formal network has been established between the 16 Catholic schools that are currently participating in the IDEAS project. These and other schools around the country using IDEAS have created a larger network which provides an environment for exploring the approach.

St Monica's participates in an international 'sister school' relationship with Tezukayama Primary School in Nara City, Japan. Communication between these schools has supported St Monica's Japanese Language Program. A visit by 22 students from their 'sister school' in 2006 strengthened the relationship and gave students from both schools the opportunity to further their language skills and learn about a different culture.

The school has a strong relationship with its parent community, which is established when their children enter school at St Monica's. Each year, the school invites parents of children entering compulsory schooling to come together as a group and assists in organising social activities. These are chosen by the parent group and may include social evenings, parent meetings or exercise classes.

The high level of social capital has been credited with assisting the school in winning regional fundraising competitions. An annual fête run by the school and its community provides a high level of locally-raised funds. The school community has assisted St Monica's by participating in the 'Shop for your School' competition that is run annually by the Westfield Group. St Monica's won first prize in 2005 and 2006, providing over AU$15,000 worth of ICT equipment on each occasion.

There is a current misalignment between the high level of innovative planning and professional development for staff at St Monica's and the design of the buildings. The school was built around 30 years ago and many of the buildings remain substantially unchanged. The school has worked with the CEO to prepare a School Master Plan, which involves the refurbishment of all work areas in the school to better align these facilities with learning in the twenty-first century.

A new school wing consists of five classrooms for Years 5 and 6. Each classroom is clearly visible through sliding glass doors and all can be opened up to a large area. An open plan will provide students with quiet areas and access to books, ICT and other resources designed to nurture research skills and collaborative learning. Funds for this work come from the Australian Government through its Investing in Our Schools Programme (AU$500,000), Catholic Education (AU$30,000) and locally-raised funds (AU$126,000).

St Monica's illustrates the benefits that can be achieved when a school grounds its strategic planning in the concept of alignment and focuses on the success of all students. Under Mary Dorrian's leadership, there has been substantial investment in professional development to ensure that all staff are at the forefront of professional knowledge. It continues to develop high levels of both spiritual and social capital, with the latter an important factor in ensuring students have access to technology and new facilities that align with pedagogical change. Alignment is evident in the adoption of the IDEAS approach.

Maria Luisa Bombal School (MLBS) in Santiago

The Maria Luisa Bombal School (MLBS) is located in the commune (municipality) of Vitacura, a suburb of Santiago, the largest city in Chile. While constitutional powers to make laws and set policies in relation to education lie with the national government, the administration of schools is a municipal responsibility.

In 2006 there were 520 students at MLBS, from pre-school to senior secondary, with one class for each of the 14 grades. It was established as a primary school in 1958, with the addition of a pre-school in 1991 and secondary years from 2000. A distinctive feature is that its governing body consists of the teachers at the school, one of only five schools in Chile to be governed in this way. The school submitted a successful bid to the municipality for such an arrangement, with the legal entity being a Public Educational Corporation. The school has autonomy in respect to curriculum, pedagogy, finance and administration. It is therefore a publicly-funded self-managing school. The principal is Nilda Sotelo Sorribes, who provided the information for this study.

While Vitacura is a higher socio-economic community, significant numbers of students at MLBS come from lower socio-economic families and 20 per cent of students have a disability (neurological 7.1 per cent, emotional 5.4 per cent, learning 5.4 per cent and language 2.1 per cent). A majority (65 per cent) come from the local commune, meaning that approximately one-third travel from other communes to attend the school. Classes commence at 8 am and conclude at 4 pm. It was only towards the end of the 1990s that full school days were introduced in Chile, and many have yet to adopt the arrangement.

The school has been highly successful on a number of indicators. It has received the Academic Excellence Award of the Ministry of Education on four successive occasions. This provides a monetary reward to members of staff. The school was one of the first in the country to receive the prestigious certificate of quality in management awarded by Fundación Chile. It is the top ranked school in the commune in student achievement at fourth and eighth grade and achieves well above national average scores in key learning areas at fourth, eighth and tenth grade. At completion of high school, seventy-two per cent proceed to university or higher education, eleven per cent to intensive preparation programmes for university selection, and eighteen per cent proceed directly to employment.

Of particular interest is the special arrangement for governance, the initiative for which was taken by the municipal authority led by the mayor. Nine months elapsed from the preparation of the proposal to the disengagement of teachers from their contract with the municipality. A committee of teachers prepared the proposal, which included administrative and financial arrangements. Legal services were provided by the commune. The Public Educational Corporation consists of the 32 teachers at the school, who are the stockholders and partners in the enterprise, with each teacher holding one share. The corporation appoints a Board of Directors, consisting of three teachers who serve a two-year term. All policies for the school are approved by the board. The arrangement commenced in March 2002.

The school has a clearly articulated mission to 'give a scientific-humanistic education of excellence, oriented toward higher education and the creation of people with visions of the future'. Attitudes to be inculcated include self-responsibility, self-respect, honesty, solidarity, freedom, love and equality. This school is highly strategic in the way it goes about its work, with its own models for curriculum planning and quality assurance, including performance evaluation of teachers.

The organisational structure resembles a private school more than a public school. The principal has responsibility for implementation of every aspect of the school's operations, which are organised on a project basis. There are six areas of operation: administration and finance, curriculum and pedagogy, teaching, research and training, family counselling, and behaviour and conduct regulations. The school receives a grant from the Ministry of Education and the municipality to operate the school, with the latter providing the larger share. The initial capital of the corporation in 2002 was US$5,926. It was US$215,205 in 2006.

Principal Nilda Sotelo Sorribes described the advantages of the approach. The school designs its own curriculum and approaches to teaching and learning, but generally follows the programmes of the Ministry of Education. The school also offers its own complementary programmes in an extended school day. The organisational arrangements reflect the priorities of the school. The profiles for every position are designed by the school. Staff are contracted to the school and are assured the same salaries, professional development opportunities and other benefits as their counterparts elsewhere in public education but, in addition, receive bonuses for reaching pedagogical and administrative targets and special bonuses for national holidays. Professional development is fully funded. Where income exceeds expenditure, profits are allocated to projects to support the achievement of higher academic standards. Some may be distributed to staff.

All services that are not directly related to teaching and learning are outsourced, including accounting, legal, cleaning and security. Brian Caldwell visited the school in 2005 and noted, in particular, the exceptional cleanliness of the school and its grounds. Expert consultants are employed to provide support to staff in areas of the curriculum where improvement in teaching and learning is sought. A consulting company is employed to evaluate programmes in English, languages, mathematics and science. Additional funds have been obtained from a range of foundations and these have been allocated to science laboratories, the media centre and learning resource centre. Professional development is intensive and targeted at areas of high priority for the school. Arrangements are made with a range of community organisations for the use of sporting facilities.

A high degree of alignment is evident among the four forms of capital, made effective through its unusual approach to governance. Some observers, on initially learning of the arrangement wherein the governing body and shareholders are the teachers themselves, might expect the school to be inward looking, with the most powerful alignment to be found between the policies approved by the board and narrowly-defined professional interests. Instead, one finds a high level of social capital, indicated by the alignment of school programmes and a national framework, complemented by local design that reflects the interests and aspirations of students and their parents. Support is sought from a range of public and private sources, with surpluses (profits) ploughed into the further development and refinement of academic programmes but also shared among staff. Intellectual capital is made strong with powerful professional development programmes for teachers but also the outsourcing of particular functions to expert consultants. Talent force and outsourcing initiatives along the lines described in Chapter 4 are evident at MLBS. Spiritual capital is strong as far as a unifying set of values is concerned. Everything is geared to providing the best possible outcomes for all students, with success indicated in Ministry of Education awards and comparisons with like schools. The quality of its governance, leadership, management and administration is indicated in the school being an early recipient of certification by Fundación Chile.

Park High School in London

Park High School is in the London Borough of Harrow and has 1,120 students aged 12 to 16. Since 2002 it has offered a specialism in technology, with a sixth form added in 2007. It is a multicultural school with about 40 languages spoken, although most students speak English fluently. The largest ethnic group, about 60 per cent of students, is Asian. About 8 per cent of students (just less than half the national average) receive Free School Meals (FSM), and the proportion with Special Education Needs (SEN) is about the national average. In 2006, 74 per cent of students received at least 5 A*–C grades at GCSE, most including English and mathematics, which is a record high for the school. As a result, the school has been described by the Department for Education and Skills (DfES) as one of the most improved and successful in London. The school is significantly oversubscribed.

The school has been selected as a study of success because of the outstanding quality of its governance, as assessed by Ofsted in March 2006; the evolution of a student-focused planning model; the systematic efforts to build the intellectual and social capital of the school; and the contributions these developments are making to improvement in learning outcomes.

The school is aware of the need to meet challenging national targets on pupil achievement but is keen to do so in a way that supports students as lifelong learners. Managing this dilemma is the key leadership concern and is included in the school's strategic aims. There were two key thrusts for school development in 2005 and 2006: (1) the development of the school's tracking of individual pupil progress, and the effective use of this both by teachers in the classroom and by those in curriculum leadership roles; and (2) the deepening of teachers' understanding of how students learn, and how 'deep learning' can be supported throughout the school. Supporting both these developments are two major strengths of the school recognised by Ofsted: the influence of 'student voice' and the extent and quality of professional development for teachers. The Ofsted report of March 2006 included the following observations:

> The school is very well led and managed. The headteacher [Tony Barnes] has an innovative and successful approach to raising standards. For example, the "Building Learning Power" [based on a programme developed by Guy Claxton] and the staff professional development programme are beginning to raise achievement across the school. These initiatives have focused the school's attention on improving learning for all students. The way in which the governing body has been involved in these developments is an example of their outstanding work. They provide challenge, rigour and a clear strategic direction. The headteacher is well supported by a very able senior leadership team. Resources are used well. The whole school community is effectively consulted on key issues.
>
> (Ofsted, 2006)

A feature of governance, explained Tony Barnes, is the systematic approach to planning, with senior staff preparing review and planning papers, each up to five pages in length, which guide the work of staff but also serve as reports to the governing body. A common format is emerging for these papers: context and review of the previous year, strengths, weaknesses and priorities and targets.

The school's Review and Planning Paper 13, prepared in February 2006 prior to the inspection in March, was concerned with equity. It summarised past efforts and described the new Contextualised Value-Added (CVA) data base on student achievement which had different classifications: all learners; girls at three levels of prior attainment; boys at three levels of prior attainment; and learners classified according to Free School Meals, Special Education Needs, first language of English, and ten different ethnic groups. A student-focused approach means that there is more effective tracking of progress for all students. Particular students were identified for support through a coaching initiative at Key Stage 4. Plans were made for staff development on the impact of social class on underachievement and provision of one-to-one support for students with particular needs, even if they are not on the SEN register.

Review and Planning Paper 20 was prepared in May 2006 following the inspection. It summarised strengths, as identified in the inspection report, and areas where improvement was required. Priorities for action were prepared, with particular attention being given to a more systematic approach to review. A review and planning paper on teaching quality, one of 21 to be scheduled for 2006–2007, was considered by governors in October 2006.

The school has a four-year improvement plan that is updated each year. It is summarised on an A4 page and this makes it readily accessible to staff and other stakeholders. Strategies and targets are set in three areas: pupil outcomes; learning and teaching and leadership, management and professional development. The wider context is the school's plan for the allocation of resources. A more detailed document that maps past, current and future plans for improvement is also prepared using a format developed by Professor David Hopkins.

John Wise, Chair of Governors, who acknowledges the value of the review and planning papers, explained the approach to governance that was rated so highly in the Ofsted report:

> Governors understand that they are there to set the strategic direction for the school, to oversee planning and major strategic decisions and to be accountable for statutory duties and financial responsibilities. They are there ultimately to hold the headteacher and his staff accountable, but not to interfere in the management and organisation of the school. This leaves the Governing Body free to focus on the governance issues that are really important and to make their contribution to a successful school without being distracted by unnecessary detail.
>
> (Wise, 2006)

In view of the outstanding governance, as assessed by Ofsted, we invited Tony Barnes to complete a self-assessment of governance at the school using the instrument in Appendix 3. His rating was 81 per cent, well above the mean rating of participants in four workshops conducted in England in April 2006 and close to the high score of 86 (see Table 5.1 in Chapter 5). Governance at Park High may thus be considered benchmark practice.

The way forward

There are different configurations in the successful alignment in the five schools described in the preceding pages. The Australian Mathematics and Science School demonstrates alignment of curriculum, pedagogy, the design of school buildings and personalising learning. It was established on a green-field site in 2003. Glen Waverley Secondary College has the same alignments, but is particularly noteworthy because the school was established in 1960 and many of its buildings have been bulldozed, with replacement by a state-of-the-art design. Moreover, alignment has been sustained for a decade. St Monica's Parish Primary School has adopted an approach to school development (IDEAS) that calls for alignment along similar lines to that employed in this book. Alignment of each of the four kinds of capital is evident, with realisation that the replacement of existing facilities is necessary if alignment is to be effective. Maria Luisa Bombal School demonstrates a rare kind of alignment in that governance and intellectual capital are perfectly aligned in the pursuit of success for all students: teachers are the shareholders and their elected representatives constitute the board of directors. Park High School has been recognised for its outstanding governance, and an important mechanism in achieving this distinction is a clear delineation of roles and the use of review and planning papers that focus unrelentingly on improving learning outcomes. In each school there is evidence of effective and efficient use of money (financial capital). There is powerful moral purpose, clearly articulated underpinning values and passionate commitment to the wellbeing of the learner (spiritual capital). These studies of success suggest a way forward for policymakers and practitioners and we make recommendations for action in the final chapter.

Chapter 11

New challenges for policy and practice

Introduction

The stories in Chapter 10 serve two purposes. One is to show how successful schools on three continents have each drawn on at least three of four kinds of capital as they seek to secure success for all of their students. Each of their principals readily acknowledges that there is more to be done in achieving transformation on this scale and also in fully utilising all of the resources that are potentially available to them. They may be stories of success, but they are still works in progress. There is a second related purpose. The stories demonstrate how far schools have travelled in barely a decade. This is a relatively short period of time in the history of public education that, for most of the countries from which we have drawn our information or in which this book shall be read, began a little over one century ago. In the context of the movement to self-managing schools, these accounts provide further illustration of the need to 're-imagine the self-managing school'. It is fitting, therefore, that we commence the last chapter with a celebration of what these schools have accomplished and an acknowledgement that there are many implications for policy and practice from what has been achieved thus far.

Drawing implications from these stories of success, and implementing the many guidelines contained in the first ten chapters, appear at first sight to be a relatively straightforward task for policymakers and practitioners. It is no such thing. Even the choice of the word 'challenge' to describe what confronts them does not do justice to the urgency of the situation in most settings. Progress is slow in scaling up across a system what has been successfully accomplished in a minority of schools. We need only to refer to the findings in PISA (Programme in International Student Assessment) to make the point. As explained in Chapter 6, Australia, Belgium, France, New Zealand, the United Kingdom and the United States are countries that are described by OECD as 'high quality' and 'low equity', whereas Canada, Finland, Hong Kong China, Iceland, Ireland, Japan, Korea and Sweden are 'high quality' and 'high equity'. In these countries there is no trade-off between quality and equity. If it can be accomplished in these countries, why not in others? If it can be accomplished in schools whose success is celebrated in Chapter 10, and others chosen for illustration in earlier chapters, why not in all schools?

A new default position

In Chapter 9 we referred to the view of Sir Dexter Hutt, Executive Headteacher of Ninestiles Community School, that successfully addressing the needs of students who in the past would have dropped out of school must become the 'default position' as far as expectations are concerned. He was speaking in 2006 at the 14th National Conference of the Specialist Schools and Academies Trust. Addressing the same conference, former Prime Minister Tony Blair offered a vision of schools that 'remain utterly true to the principle of educating all children, whatever their background or ability, to the highest possible level'. He called for a national consensus around such a vision. We provided illustrations in Chapter 9 of how success can be secured for all students through the personalising of learning and the application of a student-focused planning model.

The notion of a 'default position' should be applied to other areas of school operations. Traditionally, the default position is that schools at a particular level should by-and-large be built and operated on the principle of 'one-size-fits-all'. Equity means 'sameness' in virtually every aspect of policy and practice. The 'default position' in staffing is a workforce rather than talent force approach and schools have little discretion about who comes to work for them. There are few opportunities for rewards and incentives for outstanding professional practice. Direction and support are typically provided in a hierarchical and bureaucratic arrangement. There is little outsourcing.

Another area is concerned with what Fullan, Hill and Crévola (2006) describe as 'precision' in the gathering and utilisation on a daily basis of data about student readiness and progress in learning (see Chapter 9). Traditionally, whether such data were gathered and how they were used was a matter for judgement by individual teachers. In too many settings this is still the 'default position'. Richard Elmore highlights the limitations in this way:

'Where virtually all decisions about accountability are decisions (made by default) by individual teachers, based on their individual conceptions of what they and their students can do, it seems unlikely that decisions will somehow aggregate into overall improvement for the school' (Elmore, 2004, p. 197 cited by Fullan et al., 2006, p. 8).

The 'default position' for many school systems as far as decentralisation of authority and responsibility are concerned is still to take the centralised option and limit the capacity of schools to make decisions and mix and match their resources to meet priorities among the needs, interests, aptitudes and aspirations of their students. They limit the capacity of schools to do what has been demonstrated in the stories of success in Chapter 10.

Self-management can be the 'default position' in countries where there are cultural or political barriers to adopting the approach. An example is presented in Israel, where the government has decentralised a significant amount of authority and responsibility to self-managing schools. However, it has not worked for one group of schools, namely, those in Bedouin communities. Omar Mizel studied the reasons in his doctoral research and found that cultural factors, including the role of the sheikh, who serves as head of a tribe, and long-standing tribal traditions in relation to decision-making and accountability, were barriers to successful implementation. Furthermore, the Ministry of Education was reluctant to extend the same degree of authority and responsibility to Arab and Bedouin schools as it did to Jewish schools because of a general concern about granting them a higher degree of autonomy (Mizel, 2007).

We recommend that every proposal in preceding chapters should become a 'default position' and that traditional approaches, as illustrated above, be maintained only in special circumstances where the 'default position' is impossible. This means that the following will become the normal arrangements:

- Schools are self-managing.
- There is student-focused planning, with 'precision' in the gathering and utilisation on a daily basis of data about student readiness and progress in learning.
- Learning is personalised.
- A talent force approach replaces a workforce approach, and

schools are empowered and supported to seek out the best professional talent, no matter where it is to be found.

- Schools are not limited in where they can secure the best services, and outsourcing is encouraged when it delivers such services in an effective, efficient and timely manner.
- Schools, either individually or in federations or networks, have the authority to select staff and other services that are best suited to meet the needs, interests, aptitudes and aspirations of students and, subject to due process, have the authority to terminate services on the basis of poor performance or when they are no longer needed.
- Schools have the authority to offer rewards and incentives to staff on the basis of outstanding professional practice.

Every conceivable reason has been offered as to why such positions cannot be taken in systems of public education. In respect to selection of staff, senior officers often refer to the fact that such an approach is not possible in remote locations or difficult-to-staff schools. We contend that an exception to the 'default position' can be adopted when these conditions apply. It is also claimed that professional performance in schools cannot be objectively or validly measured, so it is not appropriate to offer rewards and incentives. It is said that such a practice will place teachers in schools in challenging circumstances at a disadvantage. We contend that these arguments do not stand up to critical scrutiny, given advances in knowledge about what constitutes good professional practice, and when the means are at hand to show improvement in learning, for the school as a whole and for each of its students. Experience in England, in particular, shows how outstanding professional practice has resulted in dramatic improvement in the most challenging circumstances. Experience in Finland shows that such practice can by-and-large be found in every school and that all students can secure success. It is appropriate in many settings for rewards and incentives to be shared among members of a professional team rather than allocation on an individual basis. The argument that teachers and other professionals in schools cannot be recognised in this way no longer holds.

We call on ministers in governments, senior policymakers, teacher unions and professional associations to set a new 'default position' in matters such as these, and deal with exceptional circumstances as they arise. We call for abandonment of the tired positions on the left and right of the political spectrum, for they do grave harm to students and society. On the left, this calls for abandonment of the view that all public/government/state schools should be built, owned, operated, funded and supported by public funds and public entities in a traditional hierarchical bureaucratic arrangement, with equity defined as sameness, services allocated from the centre, minimal discretion at the local level, and much of the community and significant stakeholders in civil society locked out of the decision-making process. On the right, the view that public/government/state schools should be wound back in favour of private/non-government/ independent schools should be abandoned, for it flies in the face of evidence in this book and elsewhere that 'high quality' and 'high equity' can be achieved even under the most challenging circumstances, if there is alignment of all of the resources available to schools and there is good governance. While the concept has its limitations, we contend that a 'third way' is needed, as evident for example in Finland and other Scandinavian and Nordic countries and, although much remains to be done, in England.

'Next practice' in allocation of funds to schools

Assuming that the 'default position' of self-management is adopted, we challenge policy makers and senior leaders in school systems to commission on a continuous basis the work required to allocate funds to schools in a way that reflects the unique mix of needs, interests, aptitudes and aspirations at the local level. In Chapter 7 we described the approach in Victoria where about 94 per cent of the state's education budget is decentralised to schools for local decision-making. This is the second major iteration of the approach. The first was an outcome of the School Global Budget Research Project from 1994 to 1996 (see Caldwell and Hill, 1999; and Levačić and Ross, 1999 for accounts of the methodology). A survey conducted by the International Institute for Educational Planning (UNESCO) found that: 'England and Victoria have the systems with the greatest level of delegation with Victoria offering the clearer and more stable needs-led funding methodology' (Levačić and Downes, 2004, p. 131).

The work in the School Global Budget Research Project was conducted at a time when there was a rudimentary data base on student achievement and limited funds to allocate to schools, as Victoria was still working its way out of a financial crisis (see Caldwell and Hayward, 1998 for an account of these constraints). A decade later, with continuing concern about quality and equity, a better data base, record levels of revenue at the state level, a change in government and a blueprint for reform (DET, 2003), the Student Resource Package Research Project was undertaken, leading to the approach described in Chapter 7, with the basis for allocation of funds to schools in 2007 summarised in Appendix 5. This second iteration comes close to what might be taken up as 'next practice' in systems that have embarked on such an approach.

We stress that this kind of work must be ongoing as methodologies improve, experience in implementation is gained, and most important, more schools succeed in transformation, securing success for all students. An exemplar in this regard is the Edmonton Public School District in Alberta, Canada that has had nearly 30 years of experience in self-managing schools. We described the accomplishments of Edmonton in Chapter 3.

The funding mechanism described in Chapter 7 and illustrated in Appendix 5 was an outcome of research in a representative sample of schools that were judged to be effective and efficient on a range of indicators. The system has played its part in ensuring that schools have the best possible mix of funds within the budget available to schools in the state. This does not mean that the same levels of effectiveness and efficiency as attained in the exemplar schools in the research project will, as a matter of course, be attained in all schools. Schools must play their part in deploying their funds in a way that addresses in optimal fashion the unique mix of needs, interests, aptitudes and aspirations of their students. The fact that many schools cannot do this well lies at the heart of concern about 'high quality' and 'low equity'.

Differences among schools were illustrated in graphic fashion in Chapter 2, summarised in Table 2.1, in the experience of Bellfield Primary School in Melbourne, a school in a highly disadvantaged setting that secured success on an important criterion for 100 per cent of its students in the early years, compared to a success rate of about 25 per cent for 'like schools'. As explained in Chapter 2, Bellfield effectively deployed its financial capital to build its intellectual capital so that all staff had the knowledge and skill to ensure that all students in the early years could read with 100 per cent accuracy at the relevant standard. It is noteworthy that the work of Peter Hill and Carmel Crévola, now updated in *Breakthrough* (Fullan et al., 2006), helped shape professional practice in many schools, including Bellfield, introducing greater precision in the acquisition and utilisation of data to guide the work of teachers. Former principal John Fleming illustrates: 'Each term I get each teacher's data about their kids and it is quite comprehensive, and we are looking to find kids who are under-performing so that we can make sure that they are on the right track' (from a master class described in Caldwell, 2006, p. 141). Securing success for all is the 'default position' at Bellfield.

There's something special about special schools

We are finding in the course of our work that some of the best examples of precision in the use of data and personalising the learning programme for every student can be found in special schools, that is, schools for students with moderate to severe disabilities. We have visited two on several occasions. One is the Western Autistic School (WAS) in the urban Western Metropolitan Region of the Department of Education and Training in Victoria. Its programmes address the needs of about 240 young learners and adolescents with Autism and Asperger Syndrome. The scale of transformation is indicated by its development from a small school in a church in the mid-1970s to one that operates on three sites and achieves its target of placing close to 100 per cent of its students in mainstream or generic special schools within three years of entry. Curriculum and pedagogy is personalised to meet each student's needs, taking account of capacity for learning.

A feature of the school under the leadership of principal Val Gill is the priority it places on building intellectual capital. Staff from WAS and similar schools in urban and rural regions can be at the forefront of knowledge and skill, with the opening in 2006 of the Autism Teaching Institute (ATI) that offers university-accredited teacher education programmes (www.autismteachinginstitute.org.au). The ATI was conceived, planned and implemented by WAS, which operates it under the leadership of a director who is an assistant principal.

Another exemplar is the Port Phillip Specialist School in Port Melbourne, which is noteworthy for the manner in which it aligns each of the four kinds of capital. Of particular interest is its approach to precision, personalisation and professional learning (the three components in the Fullan, Hill and Crévola approach).

Port Phillip Specialist School serves about 140 students and brings together on one site a range of education and health services.

It is a model of a 'full service school'. Each Wednesday morning from 8.15 to 10.00, a teacher discusses the work of each of her students in a meeting attended by principal Bella Irlicht and others, including several psychologists, a social worker, an assistant principal and a member of staff. These meetings are held with different teachers every second Wednesday so it is possible to plan for and monitor the work of each student on a regular basis. Meetings on the alternate Wednesday are devoted to follow-up of actions taken in earlier meetings. The approach at Port Phillip can be adapted to any school, no matter the size. Teachers at Port Phillip need to be at the forefront of knowledge and skill and there is a range of approaches to continuous professional learning at the school. The school networks the support of its teachers, with several experts in the private and public sectors on call to assist on any matter. These characteristics illustrate a shift from a workforce approach to a talent force approach, as explained and illustrated in Chapter 4.

Under-utilisation of social capital

A striking feature of Port Phillip Specialist School is the way it networks support from the wider community. The school was established in 1997, re-located from the South Melbourne Special Developmental School, which had about 20 students in a small, cramped house that was infested with white ants. Financial support for the former school was limited mainly to public funds. The school now attracts millions of dollars from a range of public and private sources. A Centre for the Performing Arts was opened in 2005 at a cost of AU$2.2 million, with funding from the Victorian Government (AU$1 million), the Pratt Foundation (AU$300,000) and a range of organisations from philanthropic and private sectors. The school has established a foundation to secure this kind of support, with several large events that have become part of Melbourne's social scene, including an annual breakfast for about 1,000 people, featuring leading football personalities, and a ball at Melbourne Town Hall.

We have sensed that many people associated with government (state) schools are uncomfortable with the way the school has gone about building this kind of support from the wider community, either because it should not have to do so or because it can more readily draw support because of the kinds of student it serves, thus giving it an 'unfair' advantage over other schools. There are several government schools in Melbourne that raise very large amounts of money each year, mainly from parents. These schools are either in high socio-economic communities or are selective schools, with a history of graduates who have highly successful careers.

Funds from sources other than government are excluded from consideration in determining the Student Resource Package described in Chapter 7 and illustrated in Appendix 5. This is a 'default position'. Why not change the 'default position' to one where cash and in-kind support is a normal part of the resource package for schools? This is what has occurred in England with specialist schools. By 2006, 2,602 of approximately 3,100 secondary schools were specialist schools, that is, they offered one or more 'specialisms' while still addressing the national curriculum. In order to receive specialist status and secure additional support from government, these schools were expected to raise at least £50,000 in cash or in-kind support, particularly in the area of specialism. This has been accomplished in schools in every socio-economic setting.

A major factor in securing this support has been the work of the Specialist Schools and Academies Trust, partly funded by government, which assists schools in this endeavour. The outcome is an unprecedented level of support from the wider community for state schools in England, accompanied by increased government funding. There have been improvements in learning outcomes, with gains apparently greater in schools in disadvantaged settings. Much remains to be done in this regard, but it is clear that a new 'default position' has been set in respect to social capital in support of schools that seek to secure success for all students.

A proper place for the use of data

The use of data has moved to centre stage in discussions at national, state, district, school, classroom and student levels. It was one of three major strands at the 2006 International Conference of School Principals on the theme Innovation and Transformation in Education, conducted in Beijing by the Specialist Schools and Academies Trust and the Academy for Educational Administration in China (see McGaw, 2006 for one of the keynote presentations). It was the only theme at the 2005 conference of Australia's largest educational research organisation, the Australian Council for Educational Research (see Matters, 2006 for a summary, with implications for students, teachers and school systems).

The performance of students in tests in PISA and TIMSS draws headlines around the world when results are released. These report the outcomes at national and sometimes state levels. Within some countries, students' results on standardised tests are often announced in the daily media, with schools ranked on the outcomes, either on overall unadjusted scores or with some form of 'value-added' correction. Gathering data on how well schools are doing is part of the accountability requirements in major initiatives such as No Child Left Behind in the United States. The stakes are high, as they are in England, because poor performances can mean the school must take 'special measures' to improve. The use of data in these ways seems inextricably linked to efforts to raise standards and the net effect for the profession is often experienced as unrelenting pressure and a feeling that best efforts are unappreciated, especially in very challenging circumstances, as for example for teachers who work with refugees who have never attended school.

There are some paradoxes and challenges to conventional thinking in these matters. Noteworthy is the fact that standardised testing and public release of results that enable school-by-school comparisons does not occur in Finland, which is at the top of the rankings when national results in PISA are considered. As noted earlier, Finland is one of the best performing 'high quality' and 'high equity' nations. As indicated in Chapter 3 and described in more detail by Harris (2006), there are high levels of trust in schools and teachers throughout the community. Parents are assured of a high quality of schooling for their children, no matter where they live. While well-funded, schools in Finland are not the best funded in the OECD and teachers are by no means the best paid. Critically important in explaining their success is alignment of the four kinds of capital. There is extraordinary community support for schools (social capital). Every teacher must have a master's degree (intellectual capital). Barely 10 per cent of applicants are admitted to highly sought-after places in initial teacher education programmes. Graduates are expert in pedagogy and a discipline. It is evident that teachers are able to tailor their teaching to the needs, interests, aptitudes and aspirations of all students in the absence of relentless national testing regimes.

There are some important policy choices to be made in other countries. Clearly important is initial teacher education, with the case being strong for a masters degree as the 'default position'. Such preparation programmes must give a high priority to the development of expertise in pedagogy and a discipline that will deliver outcomes of 'high quality' and 'high equity', as in Finland. How can other countries make the teaching profession as attractive as it is in Finland? A necessary measure, but superficial and unsustainable if it is the only measure, is more positive profiling for the profession. More important is what will be a long haul in some countries for building or re-building social capital in support of schools and their staff. Specialist secondary schools in England have demonstrated that a turn-around can be achieved in a decade.

A parallel development must be to shift the focus from external accountability, through standardised tests and ranking of schools, to internal accountability in supporting teachers who seek to personalise learning. We refer here to building a capacity for precision along the lines described in several chapters, based on the work of Fullan, Hill and Crévola (2006). This will require a substantial commitment of funds to develop software programmes that are teacher friendly and student focused. Several school systems are developing a capacity to monitor and report on a range of indicators for internal decision-making and, in the case of parents, the progress of students. While helpful and important, such a capacity is incomplete without a capacity for teachers to generate and utilise assessment for learning on a daily basis. This is another 'default position'.

Nothing in the foregoing calls for abandonment of external accountability or a retreat from setting high standards for all students. The commitment is to 'high quality' and 'high equity'. We are calling for a new priority on matters of internal accountability through precision in assessment for learning. This is no more than a normal expectation for the medical profession, in day-to-day health care (witness the computer-based data bank that most general practitioners now use to support personalised patient care) as well as in advanced intensive-care units in hospitals. It may be that in time the demands of external accountability will subside and what prevails in Finland will become the norm.

Who are the experts?

How will capacity be built and who has the expertise? The current 'default position' in many settings is to rely on universities and school and system-based in-service training, supplemented by conferences with well-known presenters who can attract participants. Without denying their value, it is evident from the contents of this book that we would turn first to top-flight practitioners in schools where transformation has occurred. The Specialist Schools and Academies Trust is setting the pace in this regard. Its annual conference that normally attracts about 2,000 school leaders is based around presentations and workshops by outstanding practitioners in schools that have been transformed or are on the way. We illustrated in Chapter 9 how outstanding leaders can contribute, and earlier in this chapter, in our reference to a presentation at the 2006 conference by Sir Dexter Hutt, Executive Headteacher of Ninestiles Community School. He introduced us to the concept of a 'default position'.

Educational and organisational theory is generally sound. There is little about leadership, planning, resource allocation and the management of change in the accounts in preceding chapters that is not explained by good theory. It is the way this theory has been applied by the best practitioners, either implicitly or explicitly, that warrants a central place for their engagement, particularly through master classes (see Caldwell, 2006 for examples of how outstanding leaders can share their knowledge in master classes). These can be facilitated by academics who know the theory, know what questions to ask, and how to assist participants to draw implications for their work settings. We are fortunate to have colleagues in the academic world whose publications and presentations seamlessly weave good theory and good practice. It is important, of course, that academic staff continue to conduct research on these developments and so inform good policy and good practice.

Outstanding work by skilled practitioners at the school level does not happen in a vacuum or by itself. In most cases it has been made possible by visionary leaders and facilitating frameworks at the system level. 'System leaders' in the traditional sense can also contribute through master classes.

Another approach that is now gathering strength is the participation of teachers and their leaders and, increasingly, students in local, national and international networks. The success of the networked learning communities of the National College for School Leadership (NCSL) and the ongoing initiatives in networking by the Specialist Schools and Academies Trust (SSAT), including its project in International Networking for Educational Transformation (iNet), are high profile exemplars. Others of lower profile are flourishing, including local networks and clusters, the purpose of which is to share knowledge, solve problems and pool resources.

How important are coaching and mentoring in the developing of capacity at school and system levels? We believe these can make a valuable contribution, but we offer a qualification. It is vital that those who coach have a record of success in transformation along the lines described and illustrated in this book. Without questioning the value of their contributions in the past, or how well-regarded they might be in a personal sense, coaching should not be seen as a sinecure for long service. The tenets of good coaching must be evident and these are described by Jan Robertson, Director of the London Centre for Leadership in Learning, in *Coaching Leadership*. We highlight, in particular, the importance of what she calls 'boundary-breaking principles' in coaching: 'The incorporation of boundary-breaking principles into the way coaches and leaders work together provides the challenge necessary to move leaders from inaction to action, from reactive to proactive, and from perpetuating the status quo to challenging it' (Robertson, 2005, p. 194).

The future

The challenge to the status quo is the challenge of securing success for all students in all settings. Different imagery has been invoked to describe that challenge: 'transformation', 'raising the bar and narrowing the gap', achieving 'high quality' and 'high equity', and moving 'from good to great'. There is general acceptance that things must be done differently in the future, and another concept has been introduced, namely, 'next practice'. We have used it in several places. It refers either to the kinds of practice that will be required if schools and school systems are to rise to the challenge, or to the kinds of practice that will be made possible with advances in knowledge. The search for 'next practice' is made difficult by the extraordinary changes that are occurring in the wider environment, whether it is the general trend to globalisation, or changes in particular areas such as technology.

Good work has been done in efforts to describe what lies in store for schools. Perhaps the best known is the formulation by OECD of six scenarios for the future of schools (OECD, 2001a). These took account of trends in the broader environment. Another example is the work in England by the Teaching and Learning in 2020 Review Group (2006). The brief was to 'establish a clear vision of what personalised teaching and learning would look like in our schools in

2020' (p. 2). That vision is one in which 'aspirations are realised for all children and young people' (p. 6). The elements of the vision include:

- A child's chances of success are not related to his or her socio-economic background, gender or ethnicity.
- Education services are designed around the needs of each child, with the expectation that all learners achieve high standards.
- All children and young people leave school with functional skills in English and mathematics, understanding how to learn, think creatively, take risks and handle change.
- Teachers use their skills and knowledge to engage children and young people as partners in learning, acting quickly to adjust their teaching in response to pupils' learning.
- Schools draw in parents as their child's co-educators, engaging them and increasing their capacity to support their child's learning (Teaching and Learning in 2020 Review Group, 2006, p. 6).

While the report refers to a critically important resource, namely, the quality of teaching and the importance of outstanding continuing professional development, there is a need for a more comprehensive and coherent view of what is required. We have endeavoured in this book to show how such a vision can be realised by aligning all of the resources available to schools and school systems and making them effective through good governance.

It's time to raise the stakes

It will be disappointing if it takes until 2020 to realise this vision. Writing 28 years earlier in *Leading the Self-Managing School* (Caldwell and Spinks, 1992), we identified ten 'megatrends' in education, that is, broad trends that had already made their appearance and were likely to characterise developments on a larger scale in the years ahead:

1 There will be a powerful but sharply focused role for central authorities, especially in respect to formulating goals, setting priorities and building frameworks for accountability.
2 National and global considerations will become increasingly important, especially in respect to curriculum and an education

system that is responsive to national needs within a global economy.

3 Within centrally determined frameworks, government [public] schools will become largely self-managing, and distinctions between government and non-government [private] schools will narrow.

4 There will be unparalleled concern for the provision of a quality education for each individual.

5 There will be a dispersion of the educative function, with tele-communications and computer technology ensuring that much learning that currently occurs in schools or in institutions of higher education will occur at home and in the workplace.

6 The basics of education will be expanded to include problem-solving, creativity and a capacity for life-long learning and re-learning.

7 There will be an expanded role for the arts and spirituality, defined broadly in each instance; there will be a high level of 'connectedness' in the curriculum.

8 Women will claim their place among the ranks of leaders in education, including those at the most senior levels.

9 The parent and community role in education will be claimed or reclaimed.

10 There will be unparalleled concern for service by those who are required or have the opportunity to support the work of schools.

Item 4 in this list lies at the heart of a vision of personalising learning. Yet, as the OECD analysis of results in PISA reveals, countries where many readers of this book reside, including our own, are still classified as 'high quality' but 'low equity'.

We believe it is time to raise the stakes in the transformation of schools. Governments around the world have subscribed for decades to a view that a quality education should be provided to all students, but nations still fall short of its achievement, except in a relatively small number of schools. It is time for delivery to be an issue on which governments stand or fall. There are reservoirs of resources that have not been drawn on to the extent that is possible or desirable because of the limited view that is held about the support of public education. If the reservoirs of resources are considered to be forms of capital, then it is time that we increased the capital of schools: financial capital, intellectual capital, social capital and spiritual capital. It is time that every individual, organisation and institution became a stakeholder. Researchers, policymakers and practitioners must work more closely in networking knowledge about how transformation can be achieved. Programmes for school improvement are important, but it is time to raise the stakes and move from satisfaction with improvement to accepting the challenge to transform. There is too much at stake to aim for less if we are concerned for the wellbeing of all learners who are the global citizens of the future.

Appendix I

Principles of resource allocation for student-focused self-managing schools

First principles

1 A transformation in approaches to the allocation and utilisation of resources is required if the transformation of schools is to be achieved.
2 The driving force behind the transformation of schools and approaches to the allocation of resources is that henceforth the most important unit of organisation is the student, not the classroom, not the school and not the school system. It is a pre-requisite that schools be self-managing.
3 Exclusive reliance on a steadily increasing pool of public funds, with much of the effort focused on mechanisms for the allocation of money, will not achieve transformation.
4 While there is increasing recognition of their importance, there are currently few accounts of good practice in building intellectual and social capital in schools and it is important that new approaches to the allocation and utilisation of resources as well as to governance take account of their value.
5 Next practice in providing resources to schools must take account of the rise of philanthropy and social entrepreneurship.

Core principles

1 Approaches to the acquisition, allocation and utilisation of resources should conform to criteria for good governance in respect to purpose, process, policy and standards.
2 There should be zero tolerance of practices that may lead to corruption in matters related to the acquisition, allocation and utilisation of resources.

3 Quality of teaching is the most important resource of all, and school systems and other organisations and institutions should place the highest priority on attracting, preparing, placing, rewarding and retaining the best people for service in the profession.

4 Schools should have the authority to select and reward the best people in matching human resources to priorities in learning and teaching and the support of learning and teaching.

5 A human resource management plan is a necessary component of the school plan for the acquisition, allocation and utilisation of resources.

6 A knowledge management plan to ensure that all staff reach and remain at the forefront of professional knowledge is a necessary component of plans to achieve transformation, and resources must be allocated to support its implementation.

7 There should be a plan for systematically building the social capital of the school, with provision for participation in and contribution to networks of support in a whole-of-government and whole-of-community approach.

8 Principals and other school leaders should have salary packages that reflect the complexities of their roles, and be resourced for full executive and managerial support, with state-of-the-art systems to eliminate unnecessary paperwork.

9 Most schools should be re-built or replaced to provide facilities appropriate for learning in the twenty-first century, recognising that these are required to attract and retain the best people in the profession.

10 Formula funding remains the largest component of resources to support schools, but more work is needed to base per capita and needs-based elements on best practice in transformation rather on historical patterns that reflect old enterprise logic.

Enduring principles

1 Governing bodies should operate to the highest standards of corporate governance. Priority should be placed on, and resources committed to, the assessment and development of capacity to achieve them.

2 Leaders and managers in schools should operate to the highest standards of practice in acquiring, allocating and utilising resources. Such practice should be student focused, data-driven,

evidence-based and targeted-oriented. Priority should be placed on, and resources committed to, the assessment and development of capacity to achieve these standards.

3   Clarity and consensus is required in establishing complementary roles and responsibilities for governing bodies and principal.

4   Consistent with the contemporary view of transformation and its focus on personalising learning, the student should be the most important unit of analysis in all matters related to governance and the acquisition, allocation and utilisation of resources.

5   While legal action is likely to increase with the focus on personalising learning, it will be pre-empted to the extent that the highest standards of governance and practice in the management of resources are achieved.

Self-assessment of knowledge management[1]

In the table opposite, circle the number that best matches your rating of the performance of your school for each indicator. Enter the total for each domain and for all domains in the boxes provided.

---

1 Adapted with permission from Rajan, A. et al. (1999) *Good Practices in Knowledge Creation and Exchange*. Tunbridge Wells: Create.

DOMAIN	ELEMENT	INDICATOR	ITEM	PERFORMANCE [CIRCLE]	TOTAL
Systems	Benchmarking	We identify and implement outstanding practice observed in or reported by other schools, especially those in similar circumstances, with appropriate adaptation to suit our setting	1	1 2 3 4 5 Low High	
	Internet and intranet	We use technologies across the school to assist the knowledge sharing process	2	1 2 3 4 5 Low High	
	Search capacity	We have built a substantial, systematic and sustained capacity for acquiring and sharing knowledge	3	1 2 3 4 5 Low High	
	Coordination	We assign responsibility for coordinating the sharing of professional knowledge across the school and within its departments or units	4	1 2 3 4 5 Low High	
	Selection of staff	We ensure that new staff subscribe to values conducive to knowledge sharing	5	1 2 3 4 5 Low High	
	Capacity building	We ensure that building a capacity for knowledge sharing is included in professional development	6	1 2 3 4 5 Low High	
	Endorsement	Senior staff actively endorse knowledge management in the school	7	1 2 3 4 5 Low High	

(Continued overleaf)

DOMAIN	ELEMENT	INDICATOR	ITEM	PERFORMANCE [CIRCLE]	TOTAL
	Networking	We bring our staff together with those in other schools in face-to-face meetings, video conferences, intranet or internet to share knowledge about or demonstrate different approaches to professional practice	8	1 2 3 4 5 Low High	
	Communities of practice	We encourage self-organised groups in which staff exchange ideas on common issues, practices, problems and possibilities	9	1 2 3 4 5 Low High	
	Rewards	We recognise and reward teamwork among our staff	10	1 2 3 4 5 Low High	
	Appraisal	Performance in the sharing of knowledge is addressed in staff appraisal	11	1 2 3 4 5 Low High	
	Metrics	We measure the impact of knowledge management in the school	12	1 2 3 4 5 Low High	
	Budget	We ensure that adequate funds are set aside in the school budget to support knowledge management	13	1 2 3 4 5 Low High	

		#	Statement	Rating
	Balanced scorecard	14	We ensure that the impact of knowledge management is assessed in terms of student learning, professional growth, value for money and other outcomes	1 2 3 4 5 Low High
Values	Vision	15	We have aligned practice in knowledge management with the vision for the school	1 2 3 4 5 Low High
	Rights and responsibilities	16	We ensure that staff see the school as a community in which they have rights and responsibilities	1 2 3 4 5 Low High
	Champions	17	Our senior staff serve as champions for knowledge management	1 2 3 4 5 Low High
	Recognition	18	We praise individuals for exemplary work in knowledge management	1 2 3 4 5 Low High
	Mentoring and coaching	19	We engage in a personalised approach in assisting staff to perform at their best for themselves and for the school	1 2 3 4 5 Low High
	Teamwork	20	We encourage staff to work together and pool their knowledge on professional practice	1 2 3 4 5 Low High
	Innovation	21	We provide opportunities for staff to innovate in their professional practice	1 2 3 4 5 Low High

(Continued overleaf)

DOMAIN	ELEMENT	INDICATOR	ITEM	PERFORMANCE [CIRCLE]	TOTAL
	Challenge	We encourage staff to develop a 'can-do' approach to their work, even under the most challenging circumstances	22	1 2 3 4 5 Low High	
	Tolerance	We support a 'no-blame' culture which accepts that innovations often fail	23	1 2 3 4 5 Low High	
	Recognition	We ensure that good knowledge management practice is recognised	24	1 2 3 4 5 Low High	
	Immediate feedback	We ensure that staff receive immediate feedback on their work	25	1 2 3 4 5 Low High	
	Constructive feedback	We ensure that feedback to staff provides a basis for action	26	1 2 3 4 5 Low High	
	Pooling ideas	We develop a pool of ideas that can be utilised in the future even if they are not immediately practical	27	1 2 3 4 5 Low High	
	Values in practice	We survey staff for their views on how these values (items 15–27) are reflected in practice at the school	28	1 2 3 4 5 Low High	

Behaviours				
Learning through action	We arrange work in ways that encourages professional learning through action	29	1 2 3 4 5	Low High
New language	We are moving away from high specialised terminology toward universally recognised vocabulary on professional matters	30	1 2 3 4 5	Low High
Absence of jargon	We avoid ambiguous, meaningless terms which cause confusion and irritation	31	1 2 3 4 5	Low High
Learning from success	We publicise successful experiences that people can learn from rather than rely on books or reports	32	1 2 3 4 5	Low High
Metaphors and symbols	We use imagery in words or pictures to stimulate action	33	1 2 3 4 5	Low High
Sharing knowledge	We make staff aware of how sharing professional knowledge will improve practice	34	1 2 3 4 5	Low High
Impact	We demonstrate how the sharing of knowledge will have an impact on the whole school	35	1 2 3 4 5	Low High
Practicality	We demonstrate that the sharing of knowledge is workable throughout the school	36	1 2 3 4 5	Low High

(Continued overleaf)

DOMAIN	ELEMENT	INDICATOR	ITEM	PERFORMANCE [CIRCLE]	TOTAL
	Reciprocity	We demonstrate that sharing knowledge will result in receiving knowledge	37	1 2 3 4 5 Low High	
	Interdependency	We ensure that staff are aware that there will be powerful professional learning only if knowledge is shared	38	1 2 3 4 5 Low High	
	Benefits	We demonstrate that the sharing of professional knowledge results in a reduction in the intensity of work	39	1 2 3 4 5 Low High	
	Legacy	We encourage staff to do worthwhile things that will have a lasting impact on the school	40	1 2 3 4 5 Low High	

TOTAL

Self-assessment of governance[1]

In the table overleaf, circle the number that best matches your rating of the performance of your school for each indicator. Enter the total for each domain and for all domains in the boxes provided.

---

1 Based on material in Department of Education, Science and Training (DEST) (Australia) (2005) *Best Practice Governance: Education Policy and Service Delivery*. Canberra: DEST.

DOMAIN	ELEMENT	INDICATOR	ITEM	PERFORMANCE [CIRCLE]	TOTAL
Purpose	Outcomes	There is a clearly stated connection between the mission of the school and intended outcomes for students	1	1 2 3 4 5 Low High	☐
Process	Engagement	Policies and plans have been prepared after consultation with key stakeholders within the school and the wider community	2	1 2 3 4 5 Low High	☐
Policy	Legitimacy	Policies have been formally approved by the governing body of the school	3	1 2 3 4 5 Low High	
	Representativeness	Policies are consistent in their application across the school so that students with the same needs are supported in the same manner	4	1 2 3 4 5 Low High	
	Accountability	Authorities and responsibilities are specified, and information is gathered and made available to provide a basis for assessing the extent to which intentions have been realised	5	1 2 3 4 5 Low High	
	Efficiency	Mechanisms are in place to ensure that outcomes are optimised in the context of available resources	6	1 2 3 4 5 Low High	☐

				Rating
Scope	Financial capital	Financial support is sought from all possible sources	7	1 2 3 4 5 Low High
	Intellectual capital	Plans include a priority on ensuring all staff have high levels of knowledge and skill	8	1 2 3 4 5 Low High
	Social capital	Plans include a priority on securing cash and in-kind support from all possible sources in the wider community	9	1 2 3 4 5 Low High
Standards	Specificity	Expectations and intended outcomes are clearly specified	10	1 2 3 4 5 Low High
	Data	Information to be gathered in the implementation of policy and plans is of a kind that will enable judgements to be made on the effectiveness of delivery	11	1 2 3 4 5 Low High
		There is a capacity to gather information about the implementation of policy and plans	12	1 2 3 4 5 Low High
		Data that are gathered in the course of implementation are valid, timely, understandable and capable of effective use in decision-making	13	1 2 3 4 5 Low High
		Data are gathered across the range of intended outcomes	14	1 2 3 4 5 Low High

DOMAIN	ELEMENT	INDICATOR	ITEM	PERFORMANCE [CIRCLE]	TOTAL
		Approaches to the gathering of data are designed to ensure accuracy	15	1 2 3 4 5 Low High	
		There are incentives in place to ensure that data are gathered and utilised in the manner intended	16	1 2 3 4 5 Low High	
		Data are used in making decisions in the formulation of policy and plans and in making judgements about their effectiveness	17	1 2 3 4 5 Low High	
	Transparency	Information about policies and plans is readily available to all stakeholders, as is information about implementation, having due regard to the ethical use of such information	18	1 2 3 4 5 Low High	
	Replication	Implementation is likely to be successful in similar circumstances in the future	19	1 2 3 4 5 Low High	
	Ownership	There is a strong sense of commitment on the part of stakeholders to policy and plans as well as approaches to their implementation	20	1 2 3 4 5 Low High	

TOTAL

Self-assessment of resource allocation

In the table overleaf, circle the number that best matches your rating of the performance of your school for each indicator. Enter the total for each of the two domains in the boxes provided.

DOMAIN	DESCRIPTION	ITEM	PERFORMANCE [CIRCLE]	TOTAL
Process	Annual planning occurs in the context of a multi-year development plan for the school	1	1 2 3 4 5 Low High	
	Educational needs are determined and placed in an order of priority on the basis of data on student achievement, evidence-based practice, and targets to be achieved	2	1 2 3 4 5 Low High	
	Resources to be acquired and allocated include intellectual and social capital	3	1 2 3 4 5 Low High	
	A range of sources are included in plans for the acquisition and allocation of resources, including money allocated by formula from the school system, funds generated from other sources, other kinds of support from public and private organisations and institutions, and resources shared for the common good in networks or federations	4	1 2 3 4 5 Low High	
	There is appropriate involvement of all stakeholders in the planning process including representatives of sources of support	5	1 2 3 4 5 Low High	

6	The financial plan has a multi-year outlook as well as an annual budget, with all components set out in a manner that can be understood by all stakeholders	1 2 3 4 5 Low High	
7	Appropriate accounting procedures are established to monitor and control expenditure	1 2 3 4 5 Low High	
8	Money can be transferred from one category of the budget to another as needs change or emerge during the period covered by the budget	1 2 3 4 5 Low High	
9	Plans for knowledge management and the building of social capital, including philanthropy and the contributions of social entrepreneurs, are included in or complement the financial plan	1 2 3 4 5 Low High	☐

Outcomes

1	Educational targets are consistently achieved through the planned allocation of resources of all kinds	1 2 3 4 5 Low High	
2	Actual expenditure matches intended expenditure, allowing for flexibility to meet emerging and/or changing needs	1 2 3 4 5 Low High	☐

The Student Resource Package in Victoria

The Student Resource Package (SRP) is the sum of money allocated to government (state) schools in Victoria in a system of self-managing schools, in which approximately 94 per cent of the state's education budget is decentralised to schools for local decision-making. The following is a summary of objectives, features and major elements in the package. The approach is based on the findings of a research project announced in the *Blueprint for Government Schools* (DET, 2003). Details of the SRP can be found at www. sofweb.vic.edu.au/SRP.

Objectives

- shifting the focus to student outcomes and school improvement by moving from providing inputs to providing the resources needed to improve outcomes;
- improving the targeting of resources to achieve better outcomes for all students by aligning resourcing to individual student learning needs;
- ensuring the fairness of treatment of schools, with schools with the same mix of student learning needs receiving the same levels of funding;
- improving the transparency of student resource allocations by reducing complexity;
- providing greater certainty for schools about their ongoing level of resourcing, allowing for more effective forward planning;
- providing flexibility to meet increasingly diverse student and community needs and encourage local solutions through innovation; and
- developing a dynamic model that allows ongoing review and refinement based on evidence.

Features

- Distinction between student-based funding, school-based funding and targeted initiatives.
- Student-based funding is the major source of resources. It is driven by the levels of schooling of students and their family and community characteristics. It consists of allocations for core student learning and equity. Most funding is allocated through per student rates.
- School-based funding provides for school infrastructure and programmes specific to individual schools.
- Targeted initiatives include programmes with specific targeting criteria and/or defined life-spans.

Student based funding

Core student learning allocation

Component/ Item	School Type	Basis for Allocation
Per Student Funding Prep – Year 12	Primary/ Secondary	Prep – Year 2 $5,275 Years 3–4 $4,491 Years 7–8 $5,635 Years 9–12 $5,975
Enrolment Linked Base	Primary	*Flat base, reducing above an enrolment threshold* $37,527 *Taper:* Base reduces above enrolment threshold of 500 at per-student rate of: −$100.39
	Secondary	$349,088 *Taper:* Base reduces above enrolment threshold of 400 at per-student rate of: −$299.12
Small School Base	Primary <80.1 students	*Reducing base:* $25,623
Primary under 80.1 Secondary under 400	Secondary <400 students	Taper: Base reduces for each student at the rate of: −$134.02 Credit $97,878 Cash $6,039 Total $103,917 Taper: Base reduces for each student at the rate of: −$358.34
Rural School Size Adjustment Factor	Primary/ Secondary	Funding for schools in non-metropolitan, non-provincial locations. Primary schools <201 students Secondary colleges <501 students.

Equity funding

Component/ Item	School Type	Basis for Allocation
Student Family Occupation (SFO)	Primary/ Secondary	To be eligible, schools must exceed state-wide median SFO density. *Formula:* (SFO index rating – state-wide median 0.4731) x enrolment x per-student rate. Per-student rate: $1,290.41 Minimum in eligible schools: $10,000
Middle Years Equity (Years 5 – 9)	Primary/ Secondary	*Formula:* (School SFO density – state-wide 80th per centile SFO density) x years 5–9 enrolment x per-student rate. Per-student rate: $2,899 Minimum in eligible schools: $5,000
Secondary Equity (Years 7 – 9)	Secondary	*Formula:* School SFO density x years 7–9 enrolment x per student rate. State-wide median SFO density for schools with year 7–9 students only = 0.5048 Per-student rate is $781 Formula guarantees a minimum of $12,000 for all eligible schools
Mobility	Primary/ Secondary	Schools eligible are those with a transient enrolment density equal to or greater than 10% when averaged over three years. Base: $2,119 Per-student rate: $222

(Continued overleaf)

Component/ Item	School Type	Basis for Allocation
Program for Students with Disabilities	Primary/ Secondary	Based on student disabilities index: – Level 1 $5,017 – Level 2 $11,604 – Level 3 $18,316 – Level 4 $24,999 – Level 5 $31,629 – Level 6 $38,295
English as a Second Language (ESL)	Primary/ Secondary	ESL funding is based on an integrated weighted index for primary and secondary students that is applied to a school's profile of students from language backgrounds other than English.
ESL Index		**SFO Weighting** |	0.6	1.0	1.4
Level 1	$226	$378	$529
Level 2	$454	$756	$1,058
Level 3	$908	$1,512	$2,117
Level 4	$1,154	$1,924	$2,692
Level 5	$1,733	$2,886	$4,042	 A school is required to reach a threshold before funding will apply. The combined ESL and MEA thresholds are $17,401 for primary schools and $33,658 for secondary schools.

References

Australian Bureau of Statistics (ABS) (2006). *Aspects of Social Capital Australia*. Belconnen, ACT: ABS.

Bahra, N. (2001). *Competitive Knowledge Management*. Basingstoke: Palgrave.

Beare, H. (2001). *Creating the Future School*. London: Routledge Falmer.

Beare, H. (2006). *How We Envisage Schooling in the 21st Century: The New 'Imaginary' in Practice*. London: Specialist Schools and Academies Trust.

Bentley, T. and Wilsdon, J. (2004). 'Introduction: The Adaptive State' in Bentley, T. and Wilsdon, J. (eds) *The Adaptive State: Strategies for Personalising the Public Realm*. London: Demos.

Blair, T. (2006a). Address to the Annual Conference of the Labour Party. Manchester.

Blair, T. (2006b). 'Education is the most precious gift'. Prime Minister's Address at the 14th National Conference, Specialist Schools and Academies Trust, Birmingham. December 1.

Borman, G. D., Hewes, G. M., Overman, L. T. and Brown, S. (2003). 'Comprehensive school reform and achievement: A meta-analysis'. *Review of Educational Research*. 73(2) 125–230.

Bornstein, D. (2004). *How to Change the World: Social Entrepreneurs and the Power of New Ideas*. Oxford: Oxford University Press.

Brown, G. (2006). Address to the Annual Conference of the Labour Party. Manchester.

Bukowitz, W. R. and Williams, R. L. (1999). *The Knowledge Management Fieldbook*. London: Financial Times Prentice Hall.

Bunting, A. (2005). 'Secondary school design for the knowledge age'. Unpublished doctoral thesis, Faculty of Education, University of Melbourne.

Caldwell, B. J. (2002). 'Autonomy and self-management: concepts and evidence'. In Bush, T. and Bell, L. (eds) *The Principles and Practice of Educational Management*. London: Paul Chapman Publishing. Chapter 3, pp. 24–40.

Caldwell, B. J. (2003). 'A theory of learning in the self-managing school'. In Volansky, A. and Friedman, I. A. (eds) *School-Based Management: An International Perspective*. Israel: Ministry of Education.

Caldwell, B. J. (2005). *School-Based Management*. No. 3 in the Education Policy Series of the International Academy of Education. Paris: International Institute of Educational Planning (IIEP), UNESCO.

Caldwell, B. J. (2006). *Re-imagining Educational Leadership*. London: ACER Press and Sage.

Caldwell, B. J. and Hayward, D. K. (1998) *The Future of Schools: Lessons from the Reform of Public Education*. London: Falmer.

Caldwell, B. J. and Hill, P. W. (1999). 'Recent developments in decentralising school budgets in Australia'. In Goertz, M. and Odden, A. (eds) *School-Based Financing*. Twentieth Annual Yearbook of the American Education Finance Association. Thousand Oaks, CA: Corwin Press. Chapter 5, pp. 102–28.

Caldwell, B. J. and Spinks, J. M. (1986). *Policy-Making and Planning for School Effectiveness: A Guide to Collaborative School Management*. Hobart, Tasmania: Education Department.

Caldwell, B. J. and Spinks, J. M. (1988). *The Self-Managing School*. London: Falmer.

Caldwell, B.J. and Spinks, J. M. (1992). *Leading the Self-Managing School*. London: Falmer.

Caldwell, B. J. and Spinks, J. M. (1998). *Beyond the Self-Managing School*. London: Falmer.

Collins, J. (2001). *Good to Great*. London: Random House.

Department for Education and Skills (DfES) (2004a). *Five Year Strategy for Children and Learners*. Presented to Parliament by the Secretary of State for Education and Skills. London: DfES.

Department for Education and Skills (DfES) (2004b). *Removing Barriers to Achievement: The Government's Strategy for Special Education Needs*. London: DfES. Available at www.standards.dfes.uk/primary/publications/ inclusion/883963

Department for Education and Skills (DfES) (2006). *A Guide to the Law for School Governors*. London: DfES. Available at www.governornet.co.uk

Department of Education, Science and Training (DEST) (Australia) (2005). *Best Practice Governance: Education Policy and Service Delivery*. Report for the Human Resource Development Working Group of Asia Pacific Economic Cooperation (APEC). Canberra: DEST.

Department of Education (Tasmania) (2002). *Essential Learnings*, Hobart: Department of Education. Available at www.education.tas.gov.au/ocll/ publications

Department of Education (Tasmania) (2006). *Refining Our Curriculum*, Hobart: Department of Education.

Department of Education and Training (DET) (Victoria) (2003). *The

Blueprint for Government Schools. Melbourne: Department of Education and Training. Available at www.sofweb.vic.edu.au/blueprint

Department of Education and Training (DET) (Victoria) (n.d.). 'Development of the Student Resource Package 2005 and 2006'. Unpublished document available on request from DET.

Department of Education and Training (DET) (Victoria) (2004). *The Privilege and the Price*. Melbourne: DET.

Department of Education and Training (DET) (Victoria) (2005). *New Student Report Cards*. Melbourne: DET.

Department of Education and Training (DET) (Victoria) (2006). 'Guide to the 2007 Indicative Student Resource Package'. Melbourne: DET. Available at www.sofweb.vic.edu.au/SRP

Dimmock, C. (2000). *Designing the Learning-Centred School*. London: Falmer.

The Economist (2006a). 'The business of giving: a survey of wealth and philanthropy'. Special Section. 25 February.

The Economist (2006b). 'Clever red-necks: It's not just the economy that is booming; schools are too'. 21 September.

Elmore, R. F. (2004). *School Reform from the Inside Out: Policy, Practice and Performance*. Cambridge, MA: Harvard University Press.

Florida, R. (2005). *The Flight of the Creative Class*. New York: HarperBusiness.

Fukuyama, F. (1995). *Trust: Social Virtues and the Creation of Prosperity*. London: Hamish Hamilton.

Fullan, M., Hill, P. and Crévola, C. (2006). *Breakthrough*. Thousand Oaks, CA: Corwin Press.

Futures Vision Group (2006). *Essential Questions for the Future School*. London: Specialist Schools and Academies Trust.

Glen Waverley Secondary College (Victoria) (n.d.). 'Leading Schools Submission Phase 3'. Available from the College.

Goh, C. T. (1997). 'Shaping our future: thinking schools, learning nation'. Speech by the Prime Minister of Singapore at the 7th International Conference on Thinking. Singapore, 2 June.

Haberdashers' Aske's Federation (2005) 'Governors and governors' committees of the Haberdashers' Aske's Federation', Unpublished document of the Federation Governing Body. October.

Hanushek, E. A. (2004). 'Some simple analytics of school quality'. Invited paper at the Making Schools Better Conference of the Melbourne Institute of Applied Economic and Social Research, University of Melbourne 26–27 August (Working Paper 10229 of the National Bureau of Economic Research supported by the Packard Humanities Institute and The Teaching Commission).

Harris, A. (2005). *Distributed Leadership*. London: Specialist Schools and Academies Trust.

Harris, J. (2006). *Alignment in Finland*. Occasional Paper 1. Melbourne: Educational Transformations.

Hargreaves D. (2004). *Personalising Learning: Next Steps in Working Laterally*. London: Specialist Schools and Academies Trust.

Hargreaves, D. (2006). *A New Shape for Schooling?* London: Specialist Schools and Academies Trust.

Hill, P. and Crévola, C. (2000). 'The role of standards in educational reform for the 21st century'. In Marsh, D. D. (ed.). *Preparing Schools for the 21st Century*. ASCD Yearbook 1999. Alexandria, VA: Association for Supervision and Curriculum Development (ASCD). Chapter 6, pp. 117–42.

Hopkins, D. (2005). 'System leadership and school transformation'. Keynote Address at the 13th National Conference of the Specialist Schools and Academies Trust. Birmingham.

Hopkins, D. (2006). *Every School a Great School*. London: Specialist Schools and Academies Trust.

House of Commons Education and Skills Committee UK (2006). *Special Educational Needs Report*. London: Government Publications. Available at www.publications.parliament.uk/pa/cm/cmeduski.htm

International Institute of Administrative Science (1996). 'Governance: a working definition'. Report of the Governance Working Group. Available at www.gdrc.org/u-gov/work-def.html

Kaplan, R. S. and Norton, D. P. (2006). *Alignment*. Boston, MA: Harvard Business School Press.

Keating, M. (2004). *Who Rules? How Government Retains Control of a Privatised Economy*. Sydney: The Federation Press.

Kelly, P. (2006a). 'Clever nation notion'. *The Australian*. July 22–23.

Kelly, P. (2006b). 'Condition critical'. *The Australian*. September 27.

Kelly, R. (2005). 'Reasons for raising the bar'. Ninth Specialist Schools Trust Lecture, London. Available at www.schoolsnetwork.org.uk/resources/publications/annuallectures

Kotter, J. P. (1990). *A Force for Change: How Leadership Differs from Management*. New York: The Free Press.

Lamb, S. (2004). 'Student and school characteristics: equity funding for RAM'. Research report prepared for the Department of Education and Training. Melbourne: DET.

Leblanc, R. and Gillies, J. (2005). *Inside the Boardroom*. Mississauga: John Wiley & Sons Canada.

Lee, H. L. (2005). National Day Address at National University of Singapore (NUS). August 21.

Lee, H. L. (2006). 'The Singapore Way'. *Newsweek*. Special edition on 'The knowledge revolution: why victory will go to the smartest nations & companies'. January-March.

Lee, K. Y. (2000). *From Third World to First: The Singapore Story 1965–2000*. New York: HarperCollins.

Levačić, R. and Downes, P. (2004). *Formula Funding of Schools, Decentralisation and Corruption: A Comparative Analysis.* Paris: International Institute of Educational Planning (IIEP) (UNESCO).

Levačić, R. and Ross, K. N. (eds). (1999). *Needs-Based Resource Allocation in Education via Formula Funding of Schools.* Paris: International Institute for Educational Planning (IIEP), UNESCO.

Linder, J. (2004). *Outsourcing for Radical Change: A Bold Approach to Enterprise Transformation.* New York: Amacon.

McGaw, B. (2006). 'Use of data in innovation and transformation in schools and school systems'. Keynote presentation at the International Conference of School Principals on the theme Innovation and Transformation in Education, conducted by the Specialist Schools and Academies Trust and the Academy for Educational Administration. Beijing 13–16 October. Available at www.ssat.org.uk

Matters, G. (2006). *Using Data to Support Learning in Schools: Students, Teachers, Systems.* Camberwell: Australian Council for Educational Research (ACER).

Mizel, O. (2007). 'Accountability and school based management in Arab Bedouin schools in Israel'. Paper presented at 20th Annual Conference of the International Congress for School Effectiveness and Improvement (ICSEI). Bernardin, Slovenia, 3–6 January.

Ministry of Education (MOE). (Singapore) (2005). *Nurturing Every Child: Flexibility & Diversity in Singapore Schools.* Singapore: Ministry of Education.

National Association of Head Teachers (NAHT) Eastern Leadership Centre (ELC), University of Cambridge, National College of School Leadership (NCSL), and Hay Group (2005). *Leading Appointments: A Study into and Guidance on Headteacher Recruitment.* Interim Report. Available at www.naht.org.uk

Office for Standards in Education (Ofsted) (2004). *Special Educational Needs and Disability: Towards Inclusive Schools.* London: Ofsted. Available at www.Ofsted.gov.uk/publications/index

Office for Standards in Education (Ofsted) (2006). Inspection Report No. 102236 of Park High School, London Borough of Harrow. Available on the website of Park High School at www.parkhighstanmore.org.uk

OECD (2001a). *What Schools for the Future?* Chapter 3 'Scenarios for the Future of Schooling'. Paris: OECD.

OECD (2001b). *The Wellbeing of Nations: The Role of Human and Social Capital, Education and Skills.* Paris: Centre for Educational Research and Innovation (CERI), OECD.

OECD (2006). *PEB Compendium of Exemplary Educational Facilities.* Third Edition. Paris: OECD.

Peters, T. (2003). *Re-imagine!* London: Dorling Kindersley.

PricewaterhouseCoopers (PwC) (2003). *Building better performance: An empirical assessment of the learning and other impacts of schools capital investment.*

DfES Research Report RR407. London: Department for Education and Skills.

Putnam, R. D. (2000). *Bowling Alone: The Collapse and Revival of American Community*. New York: Touchstone.

Rajan, A. et al. (1999). *Good Practices in Knowledge Creation and Exchange*. Tunbridge Wells: Create.

Robertson, J. (2005). *Coaching Leadership*. Wellington: NZCER Press.

Rowe, K. J. (2004). 'The importance of teaching: ensuring better schooling by building teacher capacities that maximise the quality of teaching and learning provision – implications of findings from emerging international and Australian evidence-based research'. Invited paper at the Making Schools Better Conference of the Melbourne Institute of Applied Economic and Social Research, University of Melbourne 26–27 August.

Rueff, R. and Stringer, H. (2006). *Talent Force*. Upper Saddle River, NJ: Pearson Prentice Hall.

Schleicher, A. (2004). 'I resultati dell'Italia nell'indagine OCSE "Education at a Glance" '. Paris: OECD. PowerPoint available at www.oecd.org/dataoecd/33/33/33732967.ppt

Schofield, A. (2006). 'Essential questions for the future school'. In Futures Vision Group, *Essential Questions for the Future School*. London: Specialist Schools and Academies Trust. Chapter 4.

Sergiovanni, T. J. (1984). 'Leadership and excellence in schooling'. *Educational Leadership*. February.

Sims, E. (2006). *A New Shape for Schooling? Deep Learning – 1*. London: Specialist Schools and Academies Trust.

Smith, J. (2005). 'Education improvement partnerships'. Paper presented by Hon Jacqui Smith, Minister for Schools, to Department for Education and Science, London. Available at www.dfes.gov.uk/speeches

Smithers, R. (2006). 'Headteacher vacancies expose schools crisis'. *The Guardian*. 12 January.

State of Colorado (2005). Executive Order B 009 05 Colorado Education Alignment Council, Governor of Colorado, 4 October 2005.

Stewart, T. A. (1997). *Intellectual Capital: The New Wealth of Organisations*. London: Nicholas Brealey.

Stringfield, S., Ross, S. and Smith, L. (eds). (1996). *Bold Plans for School Improvement: The New American School Designs*. Mahwah, NJ: Lawrence Elbaum.

Taylor, C. and Ryan, C. (2005). *Excellence in Education: The Making of Great Schools*. London: David Fulton Publishers.

Teaching and Learning in 2020 Review Group (UK) (2006). *2020 Vision*. Report to the Secretary of State for Education and Skills. Christine Gilbert (Chair). London: Department for Education and Skills.

Teese, R. (2003). 'Ending failure in our schools: the challenges for public sector management and higher education'. Inaugural Professorial Lecture, Faculty of Education, University of Melbourne.

Toomey, R. in association with ElkinSmyth, C., Warner C., and Fraser, D. (2000). *A Case Study of ICT and School Improvement at Glen Waverley Secondary College.* A report in the OECD/CERI ICT Programme. Paris: OECD.

University of Texas System (2006). The University of Texas Strategic Plan 2006–2015. This and other documents related to alignment in Texas available at www.utsystem.edu

Victorian Curriculum and Assessment Authority (VCAA) (2005). All papers related to the Victorian Essential Learning Standards (VELS) can be found on the website of VCAA at www.vels.vcaa.vic.edu.au

Wise, J. (2006). 'A successful governing body'. Article by the Chair of Governors of Park High School, London Borough of Harrow, in a newsletter for governors in Harrow published by the Achievement and Inclusion Service, Harrow Local Education Authority.

Woessmann, L. (2001). 'Why students in some countries do better: international evidence on the importance of education policy'. *Education Matters.* Summer, pp. 67–74.

World Bank Group (2001). 'Public sector governance: indicators of governance and institutional quality'. Available at www1.worldbank.org/ publicsector/indicators.htm

Zuboff, S. and Maxmin, J. (2004). *The Support Economy.* New York: Penguin Books.

Index